ACTIVE OR PASSIVE

A Guide to Being a Better Defender

James Marsh Sternberg, MD (Dr J)

authorHOUSE

AuthorHouse™
1663 Liberty Drive
Bloomington, IN 47403
www.authorhouse.com
Phone: 833-262-8899

Published by AuthorHouse 08/19/2022

ISBN: 978-1-6655-6823-4 (sc)
ISBN: 978-1-6655-6822-7 (e)

DEDICAZIONE

A Marco e Barbara

Di Giralimo

Grazie per fare la mia seconda vita in Italia, una esperienza incredibile

Also by James Marsh Sternberg

Playing to Trick One – No Mulligans in Bridge (2nd Ed)

Trump Suit Headaches; Rx for Declarers and Defenders

The Finesse; Only a Last Resort

Blocking and Unblocking

Shortness – a Key to Better Bidding (2nd Ed)

When Michaels Met The Unusual

From Zero to Three Hundred; A Bridge Journey

Reversing the Dummy

Trump Promotion; The Uppercut

Active or Passive – Becoming a Better Defender

James Marsh Sternberg with Danny Kleinman

Second Hand High; Third Hand Not So High

An Entry, An Entry, My Kingdom For An Entry

L O L; Loser on Loser

In Search of a Second Suit

Elimination and Endplay

Suit Preference; Abused and Misused

CONTENTS

ACKNOWLEDGEMENTS

This book would not have been possible without the help of several friends. Frank Stewart, Michael Lawrence, Anne Lund, Randy Baron, Willie Fuchs and the late Eddie Kantar all provided suggestions for material for this book.

I am forever indebted to Hall of Famer Fred Hamilton and the late Allan Cokin and Bernie Chazen, without whose guidance and teaching I could not have achieved whatever success I have had in bridge.

Special thanks to my editor and frequent co-author Danny Kleinman.

And of course, Vickie Lee Bader, whose love and patience helped guide me thru the many hours of this endeavor.

James Marsh Sternberg, MD
Palm Beach Gardens, FL
mmay001@aol.com

HOW TO BEST USE THIS BOOK

This book is divided into three sections. Part I discusses general considerations. Usually only one hand is shown.

In Part II, the book deals with Passive vs Aggressive Opening Leads. Try to select your choice of leads before looking at the whole deal.

In Part III, the opening lead is shown. Try to plan your defense without looking at the whole deal below.

A few deals show all four hands at the top for convenience.

The themes of the deals are random, following no particular pattern.

I hope you find the deals instructive and interesting. Have fun.

Jim

INTRODUCTION

Let's face it; defense is tough. Most players would rather declare than defend.

As declarer, you can see all of your side's assets and you are better able to formulate a plan. Is this a deal for developing a long suit, maybe ruffing or crossruffing, or perhaps an elimination hand? Maybe it's a dummy reversal? Or as a last resort, must you take finesses? There are only a finite number of hand types, which as declarer, you are more likely to recognize before the defenders do.

Bridge writers therefore devote a disproportionate amount of space to declarer play. But unless you are a wild overbidder, going down two or three regularly, a player is cast as the defender twice as often as he is as declarer. I plead guilty too, having written thirteen books on declarer play before writing three on defense.

Broadly speaking, defense falls into two categories, active or passive. If active, the defenders are attacking, trying to take their tricks before declarer takes his. If passive, the defenders are trying not to give any tricks away, waiting for declarer to lose tricks himself. Probably no other one factor has caused more misdefense than by defending one way when the defense should have gone the other way.

S,J. Simon addressed this in his 1946 book Why You Lose at Bridge in a section he called "Getting Busy at the Wrong Moment." The trouble is that yes, there is a right moment but it's often hard to tell when that moment comes.

In the deals that follow, sometimes only your hand and the dummy will be shown. If all four hands are shown, try covering the other two with a piece of paper while you try to solve the problem before peeking at the unseen hands. The deals are in a completely random order and the titles just for reference.

All contain a principle that can be applied to similar deals. Assume standard leads and signals, ace from ace-king, fourth-best from length, and standard count and attitude.

Terence Reese once said that the test of a good problem was that the reader should say to himself, "I ought to have got that; next time I will." I hope you find the deals provocative and stimulating. If not this time, next time "you will."

PART ONE

PRELUDE

GENERAL CONSIDERATIONS

What does it take to be a good defender? Have an expert partner? Sure, that helps but your partner can't pull cards from your hand. (Danny wishes he could but the rules won't let him). And since we defend twice as often as we declare, what's the secret?

Some days it feels like you are always defending. You never get any cards and it's easy to get frustrated. It's the rare player who ever claimed to be a good card holder. Maybe that's why Eddie Kantar's book "Defensive Tips for Bad Card Holders" is so popular.

Those are long boring days and your poor score reflects it. If you have blown tricks and let four or five bad contracts slip thru, the best you will achieve with your brilliant declarer play on the next four rounds will be a 54% session.

Charles Goren's 1974 book "Goren on Play and Defense" suggested that the prime requisite of a good defender was not so much technical skill but a sound psychological approach. He felt that the problems individual deals presented were fairly easy to solve if one had a proper basic mental attitude.

Goren suggested four precepts. He wrote that by following these, a defender would always be in the best possible mental posture.

1. Until it becomes certain that you can't, assume that you can beat the contract. As soon as the dummy appears, ask yourself what cards partner must have for you to do so.
2. Don't just be throwing and watching the cards as they go by, but ask yourself the meaning of cards as they are played. Not, for example "partner played the eight and three of diamonds," but "partner played high-low in diamonds, no doubt signaling four, so declarer has three." Goren suggested to be like Sherlock Holmes who remarked that to see was one thing but to observe was another. Was it S.J. Simon or Paul Simon who sang "People hearing without listening?"

3. Do your thinking in advance, wondering "What's likely to be my next problem?" Become a smooth player rather than one who is constantly making telltale hesitations. When you have ♣A32, don't be 'shocked' to see declarer lead the ♣7 towards dummy's ♣KJ64.

If you pause to guess---er, I mean, figure out---whether to play high or low, declarer won't imagine you were wondering whether to as Danny says, throw Ann Boleyn (the ♣Q) under King Henry's sword (dummy's ♣K). So be prepared to play a nonchalant deuce. You can join Danny in his quest to beat Eddie Kantar's record for most aces lost by ducking.

4. Try to help your partner. What may be obvious to you may not be so clear from his perspective. Take control when necessary. Signal unambiguously.

Here is an example. I led the ♡6 against 1NT – All Pass. When declarer played dummy's ♡J,

AJ

6 led   9842

my partner started his high-low echo with the ♡4, in case I didn't have a migraine headache yet. The helpful play of the nine cannot cost and cannot mislead. Like Danny says, "Don't mumble."

SELECTING A STRATEGY

Defense in TOUGH. Declarer sees all 26 of his side's cards. He is in complete control of his line of play. But defenders have a major obstacle – their partner. They must cooperate with each other to try to control the line of play.

Usually the first question an opening leader asks is: "What should my opening lead be?" But that's not the right first question. Better to ask: "What's the likely strategy to use to defend this deal? Can I hope to beat this contract or should I be thinking about trying to stop overtricks?" This will help select the proper opening lead.

The opening leader's partner should be thinking "What will my partner likely lead?" When a different suit is led, he should ask himself "Why that lead and not the suit I expected?" After seeing dummy, both defenders can rethink their goals and the plan initiated by the opening lead.

Often yes, continue but if not, a switch is usually not too late. Just because you are regretting your opening lead after seeing dummy doesn't mean you should give up. The defense can often survive one slip, but usually not two.

There are three basic defensive strategies. Active defense, passive defense, and attacking trumps which includes a forcing defense. Let's look at each one briefly, then we will go into more detail.

1. ACTIVE DEFENSE – Trying to take your tricks as quickly as possible before declarer takes his. Declarers love players who always adopt active defense. This is the defense adopted by most newer players. They lead out their aces and kings as quickly as possible, afraid of losing them. This is rarely correct, only in certain cases as we will see.
2. PASSIVE DEFENSE - The opposite, making declarer work for his tricks, trying to give him nothing. Declarers hate passive defenders.
3. ATTACKING TRUMPS - There are three types. In one, you lead trumps to prevent declarer from ruffing losers in dummy. Another is an attempt to gain trump tricks by either trump promotion or gaining trump control by shortening declarer, a forcing defensive strategy. Then at times, a trump may be a defender's only safe exit card while defending passively.

ACTIVE OR PASSIVE?

Sometimes the play is like a race. Often there are more than thirteen tricks available in a contract. Can the defenders get the setting tricks they need before declarer gets the making tricks?

Yes, on some deals, fourteen or fifteen tricks are available and the race is on. But often declarer needs charitable donations from the defenders to make his contract.

Whoever leads a suit first often blows a trick. When queen-third faces jack-third and the ace and king are divided, breaking the suit surrenders the third trick in the suit.

Mike Lawrence estimated that on average a defender who breaks a new suit costs his side nearly half a trick and ranks first among mistakes defenders make. Danny says cashing aces is defender's biggest mistake. Who is right? They both are. Passive defense is the default. If you get active, you better be right!

WHEN SHOULD WE BE ACTIVE?

We need to be active when there is a danger that our tricks may run away. So remember the auction and look at the dummy, always a good idea anyway.

Sometimes after the opening lead there will be clues. Sometimes your game plan will be obvious. Dummy may have a beautiful source of tricks either ready to run or about to be set up.

In either case we need to get our side tricks before declarer can discard his losers on that ready-to-roll suit, a typical 'fifteen trick' deal.

Sometimes it is less obvious. Even dummy's four-card side suit may give declarer the contract-fulfilling trick if neither defender has four cards in it.

WHEN SHOULD WE BE PASSIVE?

We need to be passive whenever the dummy is worthless, providing no tricks. There are suits that we do not want to break. Nothing is going away and we want to let declarer do all the work. We need do nothing but wait for declarer to lead from his hand and win our tricks cheaply, capturing his honors with our honors.

A SPECIAL CASE: LEADING TRUMP

Leading a trump can be either an active or passive play. If it seems declarer is going to be ruffing losers in the dummy, playing a trump is an active defense to decrease the number of ruffs.

If all other suits look dangerous, leading a trump may be a passive play to avoid helping declarer.

ACTIVE DEFENSE

Sometimes you will want to go all out in an attempt to set a contract. This is especially true at IMP scoring and rubber bridge. Doing this might give up an overtrick or two that you might otherwise have saved.

Other times you may want to be more passive, especially at matchpoints, to avoid giving away overtricks. But don't get carried away by overtrick prevention. Often your only chance for a good matchpoint score is to beat the contract.

Active defense may be best when the opponents have shown extra values or if the bidding suggests one opponent has a long suit which will provide a parking place for losers. Also against a small slam, an active defense is often best.

Some examples of an active defense include trying to get a ruff, forcing (tapping) declarer so he runs out of trumps, leading trumps to prevent ruffs, and knocking out an entry to declarer's hand or dummy before declarer is ready to use it.

Other active defenses include forcing declarer to ruff high so you can promote a trump trick for the defense. Also setting up a long suit of your own to be able to cash the setting tricks before declarer can discard his losers.

PASSIVE DEFENSE

The main idea is to avoid leading from a tenace that will give a trick away and avoid leading a suit that will finesse partner's queen-third or other fragile holdings.

Passive defense means avoiding plays that give declarer ruff/sluffs, extra entries or free finesses. Leading solid suits, or suits that have become solid can serve both as active and passive defenses. But sometimes the best you can do is simply to put declarer back in with tricks you cannot keep him from taking.

Remember someone once said, "Render unto Caesar that which is Caesar's." Good advice for defenders!

Here are some clues that point to ACTIVE opening leads:

1. The opponents have shown extra values
2. One opponent has shown a long side suit that will provide an ample source of tricks.
3. The opponents have bid a small slam. Often you need set up a second trick before declarer drives out an ace or other stopper to set up his twelfth trick.
4. You know honors are sitting well and suits are breaking well for the declarer.

Here are some clues that point to a PASSIVE opening lead:

1. Declarer is strong and dummy is weak 2NT - All Pass
2. Opponents have struggled to a contract 1NT - 2NT - 3NT
3. The opponents seem to have fairly balanced hands
4. Opponents have bid a grand slam or 6NT
5. You have strength, partner is very weak, 1NT – 3NT and you have 9-10 HCP
6. When you lack an attractive suit at NT
7. When you have keycards in their suits

In general it pays to make active opening leads. There is often something you need to be doing, especially again notrump contracts.

SUIT CONTRACTS VERSUS NOTRUMP

Suit contract play is very different from a notrump contract. We shall play a much more passive defense versus a suit contract. Let's see how that works.

The most important difference is that notrump is a race in developing long suits so active defense is usually necessary. In contrast, in suit contracts the declarer can control the suit establishing attempts of the defenders with his trump suit. A passive defense is played more frequently.

In passive defending, defenders lead suits trying not to give tricks to the declarer, closed suits like QJ10x. This works well because it helps the defenders and doesn't aid the declarer. Another example is leading neutral suits which are almost always available.

For example, a defender can lead a suit of xxxxx several times. If partner has an honor, he will be finessed anyhow. If not, we have given nothing away. Also in suit contracts, the third round of a suit will rarely stand up, only in cases where the suit is divided 4333.

OPENING LEAD SUGGESTIONS

The defense has the dubious privilege of making the opening lead which gives them a head start. But they have to take advantage of the opportunity. It is a burden as well as an opportunity. More contracts are won or lost on the opening lead than any other time. Even the best blow tricks on opening lead about 20% of the time, not because their leads are faulty but because their leads are blind.

In most cases, the tricks that make or break contracts are not immediately available to the declarer or the defenders. Both sides need to develop tricks to succeed. In notrump, each side seeks to establish its own long suits. Thus, most of the time... attacking opening leads.

The question is which suit, not so much which card. We want to look for an attacking lead in the partnership's longest, strongest suit. Whenever partner has bid a suit, you should be inclined to lead it, especially when partner has overcalled.

Do not let the fact that declarer has bid notrump, advertising a stopper, deter you from this. Today bridge 'authorities' preach bidding notrump at every opportunity with any excuse. As Danny says, "Stoppers, shmoppers! Any holding is a stopper if they don't lead the suit." Failure to lead partner's suit, after he overcalled for the lead often leads to partnership disharmony. And if it's wrong? Easy – blame partner.

Danny often points out that one cannot discuss opening leads in a vacuum and ignore interrelated facets. A discussion of overcalls and opening bids is relevant. Many auctions are contested. If your partner has overcalled, that's a strong indication to get active. You will usually lead his suit even with an otherwise unattractive holding in it, such as a doubleton king.

The borders between a pass and a bid, be it an overcall or an opening bid are often wafer thin. If you want to do better on defense, take partner's possible opening lead problems into account. Do you want partner to lead your suit even from a possible unattractive holding? Then BID IT. Would you be equally happy for partner to lead his own suit? Then PASS.

One choice conduces to active defense, the other to passive defense. Of course this applies only to fairly close choices, of which there are many more than most bridge players think.

For example, ♠ KQJ97 ♡ 8 ◊ 643 ♣ K762 is a much better overcall after a 1♣ opening than ♠ KJ743 ♡ Q8 ◊K108 ♣ QJ4 despite having three HCP fewer. There is a strong case to be made for overcalling strong four-card suits at the one-level and why the old Bridge World Standard proviso "A strong four-card major may be opened if a convenient rebid is available" is a much better partnership agreement than the modern (idiotic) "Never open a four-card major." This has to do with the defense almost as much as with the bidding.

Partner's suit or your suit? As West you hold:

♠ 5 3 ♡ Q J 10 8 5 ◊ Q J 9 ♣ 8 7 4 and the auction has gone:

North	East	South	West	You would be justified in leading the ♡Q as this is unlikely
1◊	1♠	1NT	P	to give away a trick. There is a prospect of establishment
2NT	All Pass			with the diamond combination a possible entry.

While an overcall is normally based on a sturdy suit, partners may often bid one spade over a minor-suit opening with a bit less. The tactical advantage of trying to shut out an opposing 1♡ response is great. Had partner overcalled 2♣, of course you would lead a club.

Note that if partner has overcalled and later doubles a notrump contract you must lead his suit. If he doubles after you have bid and he has not, he is asking for you to lead your suit.

After 1NT – all pass, should you make an attacking lead from the longer or the stronger of two suits? From: ♠ J 6 ♡ 10 8 5 3 2 ◊ K 10 8 4 ♣ Q 9

A heart or a diamond? You should lead the ♡3. Not only to try to establish more heart tricks but the ◊K may provide an entry to cash them.

Picking the correct suit is key. Then which card is usually easy. The question is do you make an aggressive or a passive opening lead?

Sometimes you will be able to anticipate whether to be aggressive or passive just by listening carefully to the auction.

For example, after an uninterrupted auction of:

1♡ - 1♠ - 2♡ - 4♠, and you are on lead holding:

♠ 6 5 4 ♡ Q 7 3 ◇ K J 6 4 ♣ 7 4 2

What should you be thinking? Aggressive or passive? Can't you picture dummy with something like ♡ A K J xxx. All declarer's losers are going on those hearts and if he needs the heart finesse, it's going to work.

You had better get to work quickly (that means now!) and lead a diamond.

Eddie Kantar pointed out that when dummy has shown a long side suit and trump support, a trump lead is desirable only if you have dummy's long suit bottled up; otherwise Eddie said it's the worse lead in the world.

On the other hand, an auction that goes: 1♠ - 2♠ - 3♠ - 4♠ sounds like declarer is going to have a lot of work to do. A passive lead will be best.

Yes, we all were taught first choice is fourth from our longest and strongest. But let's dig a little deeper. Are there other things to consider? Of course. The auction, your whole hand, the length of your suit, entries, it's not as simple as just fourth best etc. Sometimes it's often best to make a passive lead.

Some reasons to not lead fourth best and go passive include the following:

1. Avoid a suit bid by the declarer.
2. If you have a long weak suit, especially when you have no outside entry.
3. Four (or three card) suits headed by one honor or a tenace like AQ or KJ.
4. Also three and four-card suits headed by aces.

What are some safe passive opening leads? You might consider the following:

1. A worthless four (or three) card suit
2. A low doubleton.
3. A three-card suit headed by two honors in sequence.

But don't think these leads safe. Leading from two, three, or four low cards may pickle partner's trick in the suit. Take away declarer's guess for a queen. Or from KQx into declarer's Axx and dummy's Jxx, or from QJx into declarer's A9x and dummy's K10xx. Ouch, but in the long run.....

Let's look at some specific examples.

♠ 8 6 4	South	North
♡ 10 6 5 3	1♡	1♠
◊ A 9 6	1NT	3NT
♣ Q 8 7		

You don't have a long, strong suit. Declarer bid your long suit. So don't lead a heart. Leading either minor from your lonely honor will probably present declarer with an extra trick. So what's left? A passive ♠8.

If partner has spade honors, fine. And if not, declarer was making those tricks anyhow. No harm done.

♠ Q 10 6 3	The contract is 3NT. Declarer bid spades. You want to lead
♡ 8 6 4 2	as passive as possible. Which is better? A four-card suit or
◊ A 8	a three-card suit?
♣ 6 4 2	

Longer suits make safer passive leads, being less likely to help declarer establish a long suit. Lead the ♡ 6, second highest from length and weakness, or the top of a weak touching sequence, 8753.

♠ K 7 4 2	South	North
♡ A 6 3	1♣	1♠
◊ Q J 3	1NT	3NT
♣ K 8 5		

You know partner is broke or almost broke. Make a passive lead to protect your honors. A three-card suit with two honors is a reasonable alternative when nothing else is available. A lead from Qxx is far riskier than a lead from QJx. Lead the ◊Q from two touching honors hoping to catch partner with the ◊10.

♠ A J 10 6	South	North		
♡ 6 3	1NT	3NT		
◇ 8 6				
♣ K 10 7 5 3	You have a reasonable suit and an entry. Lead the ♣5.			

♠ 7 5 3	North	East	South	West
♡ A Q 10 5 3	1◇	1♠	2NT	P
◇ 8 6	3NT	All	Pass	
♣ K 9 6				

You have your suit, partner bid his suit. Which are you leading?

You probably can't beat 3NT without help from partner. There is no reason to ignore his suit. Lead the ♠3. He should have good spades since he can't have much else. Lead low, count; you haven't raised. High if you had raised.

♠ J	South	West	North	East
♡ Q 8 3 2	1♣	P	1♡	1♠
◇ Q 8 5 3	1NT	P	3NT	All Pass
♣ K Q 10 6				

You don't want to help declarer. Should you lead partner's suit?

All other suits look worse, so lead the ♠ J, otherwise partner will assume you are void.

♠ Q 7 5	South	North	
♡ 8 4	1NT	3NT	
◇ K 9 6 4 2			
♣ J 7 5			

Should you lead fourth best, an aggressive lead? Your suit is weak and you have no entry. A passive lead, the ♡8 seems best. But be ready to apologize when partner has ◇QJx and ♣Qx.

♠ 9 6 3   Another 1NT – 3NT auction. Your best suits are the minors.
♡ 1 0 3
◊ A Q 7 4
♣ K J 6 4

You might try the ♣4 hoping partner has the ♣Q. Better is the ♣9, a discouraging card. Partner will be likely to have cards in the majors rather than minors, with his five or so HCP.

♠ 8 4   1NT – 3NT, your lead (getting tired of leading?)
♡ K 6
◊ K Q 3
♣ A J 10 6 4 2

You have a good suit and an entry, a good chance to defeat the contract. Lead the ♣J, top of an internal sequence, not a fourth-highest ♣6.

♠ K J 8 4	North	South
♡ 9 7 4 2	1◊	2NT
◊ A 8 3	3NT	P
♣ 8 6		

The bidding has been confident. The ◊A is likely well placed for declarer and suits are breaking favorably. Partner cannot have much, but you need him to have a few right cards. Lead a spade hoping to find partner with the ♠A or ♠Q and a stopper in one of declarer's suits.

With the same hand:	South	North
	1NT	2NT (Natural, invitational)
	3NT	P

It still remains that your best chance to develop a trick is in spades, but with the tentative bidding, a passive ♡7 lead is better.

♠ Q 6 3	South	North
♡ J 10		1♣
◊ 9 7 5 4 2	2♣	2♠
♣ Q 7 5	3NT	

Yes, you have a five-card diamond suit, but no entry. It likely will be at least tomorrow before the diamonds are set up. Since no one bid hearts, it's likely partner has at least four. Lead the ♡J.

You are on lead with: ♠ A 8 6 4 ♡ 6 4 ♢ 8 6 2 ♣ K J 9 6 and the auction has proceeded: 1♡ - 2♢ - 2♡ - 4♡. Both opponents show good hands. Given a chance, some of declarer's losers will be discarded on dummy's diamonds.

Your spade trick is safe, so attack clubs by leading the ♣6. If you don't defeat the contract, you might well prevent overtricks.

With the same hand you hear:	1♡	2♢
	3♡	4♡
	5♣	5♡

Declarer has extra values and slam interest. A club lead is out; declarer controls the club suit. This may be one of those rare times it is correct to lead an unsupported ace (no king).

Your side may be limited to two spade tricks. Better get them before they go away.

♠ K 9 8 4	North	South
♡ A 5 3	3♢	3NT
♢ 8 3	All Pass	
♣ K 10 5 3		

It is clear the opponents expect to run dummy's long suit. If you lead from one of your black suits and pick the wrong one, an avalanche of diamonds may follow. This might be another of those rare times where you should lead an unsupported ace to see the dummy.

Hopefully, you will know what to do next. On the other hand, a case could be made for leading either the ♠4 or the ♣3. The defense may be able to run the black suit you lead but if not, partner may get in with a diamond trick to return it.

♠ 9 7 3	South	North
♡ J 6 3		1♡
♢ A Q 8 4 2	1NT	3NT
♣ 6 4		

The auction and your hand suggest an attacking lead, the ♢4.

If declarer has a guarded ♢K, partner will likely get in to continue diamonds. Whether declarer has ♢K3 and dummy ♢J105 or vice versa, this lead will work.

♠ Q 10 6 3	The contract is 3NT. Declarer bid spades. You want to lead	
♡ 8 6 4 2	as passive as possible. Which is better? A four-card suit or	
◇ A 8	a three-card suit?	
♣ 6 4 2	Longer suits make safer passive leads, being less likely to help	
	declarer establish a long suit.	

Lead the ♡6, second highest from length and weakness unless the two top spot-cards are touching.

	South	North
♠ K 8 6 4	South	North
♡ 8 4 3	1NT	2NT (natural, invitational)
◇ A 6 4	3NT	P
♣ 8 4 3		

Remember, try to avoid four-card suits with only one honor, especially on an auction where the opponents have shown minimal values. Which passive lead is best – hearts or clubs? They are identical, is it a toss-up? The opponents did not look for a major suit fit.

Chances are partner has more hearts than clubs. Lead the ♡8 and hope you don't pickle partner's holding. ♣4 anyone? Well, maybe.

	South	North
♠ A J 10 6	South	North
♡ 6 3	1NT	3NT
◇ 8 6		
♣ K 10 7 5 3	You have a reasonable suit and an entry. Lead the ♣5	

Often a passive lead is best. Let's see some examples:

	South	North
♠ 7 4	South	North
♡ Q J 10 8	1♣	1♠
◇ J 7 5 3 2	2♣	2NT
♣ J 5	3NT	P

There is a good chance declarer does not have nine tricks. Lead the ♡Q, a safe passive-aggressive lead rather than fourth best from a weaker five-card suit after the opponents have limped into 3NT. South may have eight, nine, or ten easy tricks.

You hold: ♠ K 9 6 4 2   ♡ 6   ◊ 8 5 3   ♣ K J 9 6
and hear: 1♡ - 1♠
2♡ - All Pass

Sounds like two minimum hands and a misfit. Partner has high cards.
There is no safe lead. Try the ♣6; partner could have Q42 in each minor.

	South	North
♠ 7 4		1♠
♡ J 10 4 3		
◊ K Q 6	2♣	2♡
♣ Q 10 5 2	2NT	3♡
	3NT	P

It's a misfit and South may have trouble establishing a suit. He must be prepared for diamonds, the unbid suit. A club lead would not be safe.

A heart lead would not be right as declare plans to establish this suit.

The best lead unlikely to give away a trick is.... the ♠7. This is not an attempt to set up partner's spades, but to avoid giving away a trick while attacking the outside entry in dummy to the hearts.

MAJOR AND MINOR BIAS

♠ 7 3	South	North
♡ 6	1NT	2NT (Natural, invitational)
◊ K Q 8 7 6	3NT	P
♣ K J 6 4 2		

Which of your good suits are you leading? Actually a trick question. The major suit bias tells us in the bidding that the opponents have the minors, not the majors. No suits have been bid but there are clues.

Opener doesn't often have a five-card major, but he often has a five-card minor. Responder showed no interest in a major.

So perhaps our best lead is not one of our minors at all, but a major – the ♠7.
Spades is more promising than hearts because you have a second spade. Also a 1NT opener is more likely to have five hearts than five spades.

On the other hand, had the auction proceeded:

South	North
1NT	2♣
2 Major	3NT

The disclosure that declarer and dummy each have a four-card major creates a Minor Suit Bias. Pick one and lead it. Depending on your hand, you might lead a minor, more likely diamonds in the absence of a lead-directing double of Stayman.
If you have to lead a major, lean towards opener's, not responder's, as the honor you risk pickling in partner's hand may set up a trick for you in the suit.

All right, now you should be ready for the short quiz on the next page.

Don't peek at the following answer page.

What would you lead in the following?

a) ♠ K J 3   1♡   2◊
    ♡ 6 5   2♡   4♡
    ◊ Q 7 4   All   Pass
    ♣ J 10 7 5 3

b) ♠ K J 3   1♡   2◊
    ♡ 6 5   2♡   4♡
    ◊ K J 8 4 2   All   Pass
    ♣ Q 10 4

c) ♠ K 6 4   1◊   3♣
    ♡ J 10 9 6 4   3NT   4◊
    ◊ A 4   6◊   All Pass
    ♣ 6 4 2

d) ♠ 10 3   1◊ P (You)   1♡   1♠ (Partner)
    ♡ Q J 9 3   1NT P   2◊   All Pass
    ◊ 5 4 2
    ♣ K J 9 4

e) ♠ 6 4   1NT   3NT
    ♡ Q 10 9 3   All Pass
    ◊ A J 10 5
    ♣ K J 6

19

SUGGESTED ANSWERS

a) The ♠3. An aggressive lead since dummy rates to have a long diamond suit to throw losers. If declarer needs a diamond finesse, it figures to work for him.

b) The ♣4. A passive lead. You have the diamond suit locked up. No need to open the spade suit. Which lead requires the least from partner?

c) The ♣4. An active lead. Trying to set up the hearts won't work against six diamonds, though it would be a good plan against 3NT.

d) The ◊5. When NT is rejected, there will be ruffing values. No rush to lead the ♠10. You have all the suits well stopped. Spades can wait; if partner complains, invoke Yogi's favorite excuse: "I had them mixed with my clubs."

e) ♡10. Time to go passive. Partner cannot have more than two or three points. The ♡10 requires the least from partner. Don't help declarer by leading from strength. The ♠6 risks pickling partner's spades.

PART TWO

OPENING
LEAD
DEALS

Deal 1. Explosiveness

♠ K J 9 4
♡ A 5 4
◊ 8 6 2
♣ 5 4 2

North	East	South	West
1♣	P	1♡	P
3♣	P	3♡	P
4♡	All Pass		

What should West lead?

This is a very strong auction. South's 3♡ bid was forcing. Dummy is coming down with what? A good second suit. Is it time for a passive or active lead?

When the opponents sound like they have ample values and a strong second suit, you better be ready to fight for your tricks. An aggressive spade lead is best.

The whole deal:

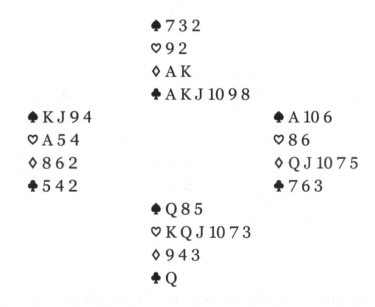

♠ 7 3 2
♡ 9 2
◊ A K
♣ A K J 10 9 8

♠ K J 9 4
♡ A 5 4
◊ 8 6 2
♣ 5 4 2

♠ A 10 6
♡ 8 6
◊ Q J 10 7 5
♣ 7 6 3

♠ Q 8 5
♡ K Q J 10 7 3
◊ 9 4 3
♣ Q

The defenders take three spades and one heart for down one. With a passive lead, declarer will make an overtrick.

What's that? Someone taught you "Never lead from a king?"

Deal 2. Two Choices

West

♠ 7 3	South	West	North	East
♡ 3 2	1♡	P	2♣	P
◊ K J 8 6	2♠	P	3♡	P
♣ 10 9 8 5 2	4♡	All Pass		

If you just listened to the bidding without looking at your hand, you might lead a diamond, the unbid suit.

But West looked at her hand and seeing the club sequence led the ♣ 10.

How successful was this lead?

How does a passive club lead compare to an active diamond lead? If partner has a diamond honor, you want to set up diamond tricks. By leading a club, you give declarer the timing to set up some club tricks to use for discards.

North
♠ Q 9 4
♡ A J 10
◊ 10 5 2
♣ K Q J 7

East
♠ J 10 5 2
♡ 8 6 4
◊ Q 7 3
♣ A 6 3

South
♠ A K 8 6
♡ K Q 9 7 5
◊ A 9 4
♣ 4

While many prefer not to lead from a king, this is a dynamic lead almost always worth considering. If choosing between leading from KJ65 and 8765, think of what you will need from partner.

With the former, only the ace or queen. With the latter, well, a lot.

Deal 3. Second Chance

	North	East	South	West
♠ Q 10 5	1♡	P	1♠	P
♡ A Q 7 6	2♠	P	2NT	P
◊ Q J 10 2	4♠	All Pass		
♣ J 9				

What should West choose for an opening lead?

West led a passive ◊Q. Passive yes but at the same time safe and attacking. Any other lead could be a blunder. This was the dummy.

North
♠ A 9 8 7
♡ J 9 8 4 3
◊ A
♣ A 6 2

Declarer won the ◊A as East encouraged with the ◊9. When declarer led a heart to his ♡K losing to West's ace, East showed count with the ♡2. Now what?

West switched to the ♣J. Declarer won dummy's ace and proceeded to ruff four hearts in hand and three diamonds in dummy. The ♠A in dummy was his tenth trick. Making four spades.

East said to West, "You had a second chance. I can understand missing the first chance but the second? Invest one trump trick to save two."

A capable defender will lead trumps in two situations. First when he wants to conduct a passive defense, trying to give nothing away, and second, to try to cut down on declarer's ruffs, an active defense.

An opening lead from the Q103 is difficult but North's jump did suggest an unbalanced hand. West had a second chance to shift to a trump at Trick 3.

South
♠ K J 6 3
♡ K
◊ 8 7 4 3
♣ Q 7 5 3

East
♠ 4 2
♡ 10 5 2
◊ K 9 6 5
♣ K 10 8 4

Deal 4. Just Don't Go First

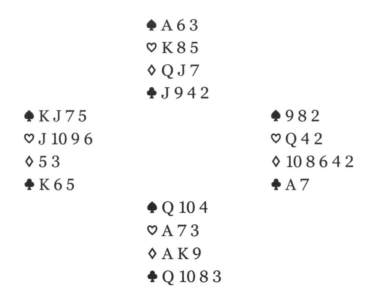

♠ A 6 3
♡ K 8 5
◊ Q J 7
♣ J 9 4 2

♠ K J 7 5
♡ J 10 9 6
◊ 5 3
♣ K 6 5

♠ 9 8 2
♡ Q 4 2
◊ 10 8 6 4 2
♣ A 7

♠ Q 10 4
♡ A 7 3
◊ A K 9
♣ Q 10 8 3

South opened 1NT and North raised to 3NT. What should West lead?
A passive heart jack or an active spade five?

A passive ♡J is both safe and constructive. A ♠5 lead is somewhat more constructive but not nearly as safe. There is no reason for an active spade lead.

Declarer wins and starts the clubs. Each time the defenders win a club, a passive heart return makes declarer do all the work.

Declarer sets up two club tricks but by not leading spades and just sitting and waiting, the defenders cannot be prevented from taking a spade trick.

Notice only East can lead spades first without losing a trick.

When declarer finally plays spades, down one losing two clubs, two hearts, and one spade.

Did your partner lead a spade?

Deal 5. Confusing Two Auctions

Evelyn

♠ 8 3

♡ K Q 10 5

♢ K J 7 2

♣ 9 7 5

South	West	North	East
1♠	P	2♣	P
2♡	P	3♣	P
3♡	P	3♠	P
4♠	All Pass		

What should Evelyn lead?

She led the ♠3. Declarer drew trumps, knocked out the ace of clubs and took twelve tricks.

"Evelyn," I asked, remaining calm. "A trump lead?"

"You told me when they bid two suits to lead a trump. What, you changed your mind?" retorted Evelyn. "That's the trouble with you, Jim. Always resulting me."

It's a good thing Evelyn didn't work in a fruit market, since she can't tell apples from oranges. Yes, after an auction 1♠ - 1NT – 2♡ - 2♠, when dummy is weak and takes a preference, dummy might provide a heart ruff.

The whole deal:

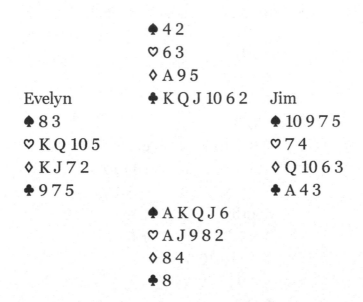

```
              ♠ 4 2
              ♡ 6 3
              ♢ A 9 5
Evelyn        ♣ K Q J 10 6 2    Jim
♠ 8 3                            ♠ 10 9 7 5
♡ K Q 10 5                       ♡ 7 4
♢ K J 7 2                        ♢ Q 10 6 3
♣ 9 7 5                          ♣ A 4 3
              ♠ A K Q J 6
              ♡ A J 9 8 2
              ♢ 8 4
              ♣ 8
```

She should have led a low diamond or maybe the king, killing the entry to dummy's clubs. Forget twelve tricks, South goes down in four spades.

Deal 6. Good Advice

West

♠ K J 5 4   North opened 1♣. South bid 1♡. When North raised

♡ 9 8   to 2♡, South bid 3♡. North wisely passed.

◊ 7 6 4

♣ A 8 7 2   What should West lead?

West hated to lead from a king. He did not want to lead dummy's diamond suit. He did not want to lead a club with an unsupported ace, So he led a passive trump, the old "lead a trump when you don't know what else to do." As you will see, the result was ten tricks for North-South.

"Why didn't you bid game?" asked South. "Why didn't you?" asked North. What was the right question? "Why didn't we beat 3♡?" asked East.

In the ACBL Bulletin, November 2011, Mike Lawrence discussed the following:

"There are times when leading from a king is mandatory:

If your partner has bid the suit. If it is an unbid suit. If your partner has bid notrump or made a takeout double suggesting values in the suit.

If you doubt me, try this: After your lead, study how other leads worked out. You will find leading from a king is a strong contender." Amen, brother.

North

♠ A 9 2

♡ K 7 6 2

◊ Q 3

♣ K J 10 9   East

              ♠ Q 10 6

              ♡ 5 4

South   ◊ A K 10 5 2

♠ 8 7 3   ♣ 6 5 3

♡ A Q J 10 3

◊ J 9 8

♣ Q 4

A spade lead sets up two tricks for the defense before the club ace is dislodged.

28

Deal 7. More of the Same

Some years ago in the ACBL Bulletin, someone wrote in to the expert writer and player Jerry Helms asking what to lead from:

♠9 5 2   ♡A 10 7   ◊K 9 7 2   ♣A 9 5 after a 1♠ -2♠ - 4♠ auction.

Since the person knew not to lead unsupported aces and had been taught never lead from a king, they had led a trump. This was not a success and wanted Jerry's advice.

Jerry agreed 100% that leading unsupported aces is almost always wrong.
"...we might consider leading a trump....unlikely to give away a trick....a passive lead. However, my preference in such situations is to be aggressive, trying to establish tricks for our side before declarer can establish enough tricks to make the contract.

The aggressive lead on this hand is a diamond, away from the ◊K, hoping partner has some help in the suit.
A 'passive' trump lead gives declarer the timing to set up a...winner to discard a... That's often the case. Given enough time, declarer will usually have the resources to establish the tricks needed to make the contract. So the only lead...is a diamond... fortune tends to favor the brave."

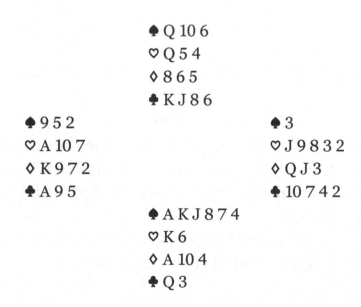

<pre>
                    ♠ Q 10 6
                    ♡ Q 5 4
                    ◊ 8 6 5
                    ♣ K J 8 6
        ♠ 9 5 2   ♠ 3
        ♡ A 10 7   ♡ J 9 8 3 2
        ◊ K 9 7 2   ◊ Q J 3
        ♣ A 9 5   ♣ 10 7 4 2
                    ♠ A K J 8 7 4
                    ♡ K 6
                    ◊ A 10 4
                    ♣ Q 3
</pre>

Deal 8. You're Up – Passive or Active?

	South	West	North	East
♠ 7 6	1♡	P	1♠	P
♡ J 6	2♦	P	3♡	P
♦ 10 9 8 7	4♡	All Pass		
♣ K J 7 6 5				

What are your possible choices? A passive doubleton spade? A passive ten of diamonds? An aggressive club six? A trump from ♡J6? A trump is much too dangerous.

West led a passive ♦10, thinking "they bid spades and I'm not leading from a king." What was the result?

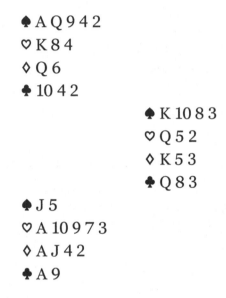

```
        ♠ A Q 9 4 2
        ♡ K 8 4
        ♦ Q 6
        ♣ 10 4 2
                        ♠ K 10 8 3
                        ♡ Q 5 2
                        ♦ K 5 3
                        ♣ Q 8 3
        ♠ J 5
        ♡ A 10 9 7 3
        ♦ A J 4 2
        ♣ A 9
```

With this passive lead, declarer had plenty of time to make his contract, eventually setting up the spades.

When you have a holding like KJxx in an unbid suit to lead from, this should be considered as a likely possibility. Either the ace or queen in partner's hand sets up one or two tricks for the defense early on, before declarer has a place to discard losers.

On this deal, South might still make four hearts even after a club lead, but he has a lot more chances to go wrong.

As Mike Lawrence says, "Never lead from a king is one of the worse pieces of advice in bridge," certainly not deserving the bad press associated with it.

Deal 9. Are You Listening ?

West	North	East	South	West
♠ 9 3 2	1♡	2♣	2♠	3♣
♡ K 8 2	3♣	P	3NT	P
◇ K 10 9 2	4♠	All Pass		
♣ 10 5 3				

Opening Lead: ♣ 10

West led the ♣10, high from three small having raised. Do you agree with the lead (not the card which was correct but the suit)? What would you have led?

Did you listen to the bidding? What do you think declarer's hand will look like? He bid the majors and showed club strength. If he has an Achilles's heel, where is it?

East won the opening lead and shifted to a diamond. Too late! Declarer won the ◇A in dummy and came to hand with a trump to discard a diamond on the club king. Declarer drew trumps and lost one heart, one club, and one diamond.

North
♠ Q 10 7 6
♡ A J 10 5 4
◇ A 7 6
♣ 8

East
♠ 5
♡ Q 7 3
◇ Q 4 3
♣ A Q 9 6 4 2

South
♠ A K J 8 4
♡ 9 6
◇ J 8 5
♣ K J 7

South's 3NT showed strength in clubs and North has a shapely hand. If the defense is only getting one club trick, an active opening lead is necessary. West's best chance is in diamonds.

With a diamond lead, the defense has the timing to get a second diamond trick. Down one.

Deal 10. Singleton or a High Card

```
                    ♠ Q 8 6 3
                    ♡ 6 5 2
                    ◇ A Q 5 3
                    ♣ 8 4
    ♠ 9 7 4              South    West    North    East
    ♡ K Q 10 3           1♣       P       1◇       P
    ◇ J 9 7 4 2          1♠       P       2♠       P
    ♣ J                  4♠       All Pass
```

Opening Lead: ♣ J

West wasn't thrilled about leading his singleton in a suit declarer bid, but how would he explain it if he didn't. Do you agree?

Singletons are at risk of pickling partner's honors. Don't substitute slogans for thinking.

East won the ♣A and returned the ♣3. Declarer played low and West ruffed. West now switched to the ♡K. Declarer won and drew two rounds of trumps.

He discarded the remaining hearts in dummy on the ♣KQ. With ten tricks, he could either finesse in diamonds or ruff two diamonds in hand, taking ten or eleven tricks.

How did that club lead work out for you?

How about a more active lead of the ♡K, trying to set up some tricks? Declarer will win and might draw trumps. But good technique suggests he might lead clubs first. If so, you will score two hearts, one club, one ruff and maybe another trick.

```
                                               East
Leading a singleton in one of declarer's       ♠ 10 5
suits or one dummy has bid is usually          ♡ J 9 7
unproductive, serving only to help declarer.   South        ◇ K 10 6
Especially leading an honor, even a singleton  ♠ A K J 2    ♣ A 10 7 3 2
jack may take a trick.                         ♡ A 8 4
                                               ◇ 8
                                               ♣ K Q 9 6 5
```

Deal 11. Too Much Noise

	♠ 4 2	South	West	North	East
	♡ 9 6 5	1♠	P	2♠	P
	◊ K Q 10 9 7	3◊	P	4♠	All Pass
	♣ J 8 2				

Opening Lead: ◊ K

West led the ◊K, happy to have a sequence and a normal passive lead. Declarer won the ◊A and returned a diamond.

"What's he up too," thought West? West shifted to a trump. Whether East won or ducked, the defense could not prevent declarer from ruffing one diamond.

Ten tricks: One diamond ruff, one high diamond, one heart, four trumps in hand, and three high clubs.

"Were you paying attention to the bidding?" asked East.

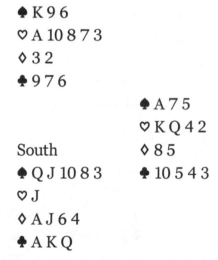

Notice that if West makes a good aggressive trump lead, East has to make a very good play and duck. If he wins the ♠A and returns a trump, declarer can ruff a diamond.

If East ducks Trick 1, West will win the second diamond and continues a trump. Now East can win the ♠A and play a third round. This deprives declarer of any diamond ruffs. Only nine tricks – down one.

Deal 12. Lots of Choices

♠ A K J 9	South	West	North	East
♡ A 9 7	1♡	1♠	2♡	4♠
◊ K Q 10 7	5◊	Dbl	5♡	P
♣ 7 4	P	Dbl	All Pass	

What should West lead? ♠A ? ◊K ? What do you think?

West led the ♠A, a passive lead. Declarer ruffed, cashed the ◊A and ruffed a diamond in dummy. He played a club to his king and ruffed another diamond with the queen of trumps.

He next led a trump. West won and led another spade, Declarer ruffed, drew trumps and conceded a diamond. Plus 550.

"Did you think about the play before you led?" asked East.

A defender's thoughts when choosing an opening lead should include trying to visualize how declarer may play the hand. This often helps choose between a passive (♠A) and aggressive (a trump) lead.

With a shapely two-suited hand, a crossruff is likely. And the defense to a crossruff? Lead trumps. Ace and another. Down one.

North
♠ 8 7 6 5 4
♡ Q 4 3
◊ 6
♣ A 10 6 5

East
♠ Q 10 3 2
♡ 5
◊ 8 2
♣ Q J 9 8 3 2

South
♠ Void
♡ K J 10 8 6 2
◊ A J 9 5 4 3
♣ K

Deal 13. Opening Lead – Passive or ?

	North	East	South	West
♠ 2	North	East	South	West
♡ K J 7 5	1◊	3♡	3♠	5♡
◊ 10 4	5♠	P	6♠	All Pass
♣ A 9 8 5 4 2				

As West what is your opening lead?

West led the ♡K, hoping to win Trick 1 and see what to do next. Declarer ruffed the opening lead and after drawing trumps, knocked out the ♣A and claimed.

East asked, "You had an ace. Did you really think we had another trick coming in the way of a high card?"

East was correct. West's lead was probably futile. Might a different lead have been more fruitful?

East had preempted. This not only promises length in one suit but strongly suggests shortness in another. West should try the ♣A.

North
♠ K J 7
♡ 8 6 2
◊ A Q J 9
♣ Q 7 6

East
♠ 4 3
♡ A Q 10 9 4 3
◊ 8 5 3 2
♣ 3

South
♠ A Q 10 9 8 6 5
♡ void
◊ K 7 6
♣ K J 10

Deal 14. A Good Agreement

♠ 8 7

♡ K Q 8

◊ Q J 10 9 5 2

♣ 6 3

South	West	North	East
1♣	2◊	2♠	P
3♣	P	3◊	P
3NT	All Pass		

Opening Lead: ?

What would you lead? Are there any inferences that might help? North's 3◊ bid was trying to get to 3NT if South had a diamond stopper.

West led a passive ◊Q.

Declarer took the first eleven tricks. Was this avoidable or am I resulting after the fact? What should East's second pass mean? Do you have any agreements?

East failed to raise. Fine but when North bids 3◊, if East has an honor- ace, king, or even the queen, he should double. This can't be length; he already passed. It can only mean I can help with the opening lead. Therefore, pass denies.

With this in mind, West should choose a more aggressive opening lead like...the ♡K and take the first five tricks. East could certainly have something even like ♡J10 fourth or fifth. Another deal with sixteen tricks.

North

♠ A K Q 10 4

♡ J 10 4

◊ 8 7 6

♣ K 2

East

♠ J 9 6 2

♡ A 9 6 5 3

◊ 3

♣ 9 7 4

South

♠ 5 3

♡ 7 2

◊ A K 4

♣ A Q J 10 8 5

Deal 15. Benito's Rule

	South	West	North	East
♠ 9 3 2	1♠	P	2◊*	P
♡ 3	2♡	P	2♠	P
◊ 10 9 8 5	3♡	P	4◊^	P
♣ K 7 5 3 2	4♡^	P	4♠	P
	5♣#	All Pass		

*Game forcing ^ Cue bid # Bid six with a club control

What should West lead?

West led the ♡ 3. Was this successful?

The heart lead served to compromise East's heart holding allowing declarer to make his contract plus.

"Why did you lead a heart?" asked East. "Benito's Rule says if you don't lead a singleton, you don't have one," answered West.

Since Garozzo is a good friend, I gave this hand to him as a lead problem.

His answer? "Un cuore? Non e possibile. Che idioto!"

Which means "Who's the idiot who led a heart?"

```
            North
            ♠ K 8 5
            ♡ J 4
            ◊ A K 7 6 4      East
            ♣ Q 9 8          ♠ 7 6
                             ♡ Q 7 6 5 2
            ♠ A Q J 10 4     ◊ J 3 2
            ♡ A K 10 9 8     ♣ A J 6
            ◊ Q
            ♣ 10 4
```

The bidding says North-South are off two quick club tricks. After three rounds of clubs, South will ruff. His logical next play will be to play the ♡AK, planning to ruff a heart in dummy. West will ruff the second heart. Down one.

- When North cue bid 4◊, bypassing clubs, South should have bid 4♠.

Deal 16. Listening?

```
♠ 9 8 7 5          North     East      South     West
♡ 8 7              1◊        P         1♡        P
◊ 9 5 2            3◊        P         3♡        P
♣ K J 6 2          4♡        All Pass
```

West is on lead. What are you leading? A trump, a spade, or a club?

West, having been taught never lead from a king, led a neutral ♠9 from his spade sequence. Was this successful? Let's see.

East asked, "Were you listening to the bidding? Just lead a club."

The opponents bid strongly. It was not a surprise dummy had a good diamond suit to discard losers, plenty of tricks if allowed time to get them. This was no time to be passive. While in this case the defense would have survived with a trump lead and a switch to clubs, generally a trump lead is a give-up play in these auctions.

```
                   ♠ A
                   ♡ Q 10 3
                   ◊ A K Q J 8 4      East
                   ♣ 9 5 3            ♠ J 10 6 3 2
                                      ♡ A 5
                                      ◊ 10 6 3
                   South              ♣ A 8 4
                   ♠ K Q 4
                   ♡ K J 9 6 4 2
                   ◊ 7
                   ♣ Q 10 7
```

Note: Was the above 3♡ forcing or to play? The actual South hand seen above or some hand like : ♠2 ♡Q987542 ◊10 ♣ J1064? That hand must pass 3◊. If you bid after an invitational bid, (3◊), you are on your way to game.

Deal 17. If Not The Ace, What?

	North	East	South	West	
♠ 9 4	North	East	South	West	
♡ K J 8 6	1♣	P	1♠	P	
◊ 10 9 8 7 6	3♣	P	3♠	P	
♣ A 6	4◊^	P	4NT	P	^ Cue bid for spades
	5♡	P	6♠	All Pass	

What should West lead?

West led a passive ◊10, knowing he had one sure trick. Unfortunately for him, that was all he scored. Declarer drew trumps and after knocking out the ♣A threw his losers on the good clubs in dummy.

What would you have led?

Let's consider the possibilities. A trump? Rarely right against a slam. The club ace? More likely to help declarer set up the clubs and it's not going anywhere.

So it's a spade, aggressive, a suit they cue bid, or a passive diamond. You will probably need some help from East.

If you lead a diamond and he has the queen, not good enough. If he has the king, it will help if it's behind the ace.

If you lead a heart and he has the queen, you have established a trick. So a heart it is. If they have the queen, then probably nothing would have worked anyhow.

```
              North
              ♠ K J 3
              ♡ 5 4
              ◊ A K           East
              ♣ K Q J 10 4 3  ♠ 7 2
                              ♡ Q 7 3 2
              South           ◊ 5 4 3 2
              ♠ A Q 10 8 6 5  ♣ 9 8 2
              ♡ A 10 9
              ◊ Q J
              ♣ 7 5
```

The aggressive heart lead sets up the setting trick before the ♣A is dislodged.

Deal 18. How Many Mulligans Do You Need?

```
                    ♠ J 9 6 5 2
                    ♡ A 9 7
                    ◇ 5
                    ♣ K 5 4 2
    ♠ A 8 4              East      South     West      North
    ♡ K 10 8 6 3         1◇        1♠        2♡        4♠
    ◇ J 9                P         P         Dbl       All Pass
    ♣ Q J 10
```

Opening Lead: ♣ Queen

West led a passive ♣Q. which held Trick 1. He continued with the ♣J which declarer ruffed. Declarer cashed the ◇A, ruffed a diamond, ruffed a club and ruffed another diamond.

Then he led the club king which East covered. Declarer discarded a heart as did West. Declarer crossruffed for ten tricks.

How many mulligans did West need to defeat four spades?

There are no mulligans in bridge. I wrote a book on that. West erred at Tricks 1, 2, and 7, any of which could have defeated the contract. Do you see how?

```
                                East
                                ♠ void
                  South         ♡ Q J 5
                  ♠ K Q 10 7 3  ◇ K Q 10 6 3
                  ♡ 4 2         ♣ A 9 7 6 3
                  ◇ A 8 7 4 2
                  ♣ 8
```

West has eleven HCP and his partner opened the bidding. How can North-South take ten tricks? Only by a crossruff. A passive opening lead - mistake number one. Where was the trump opening lead? Trick 2 - where was the trump switch?

Trick 7- ruff partner's ♣A and play ace and a spade. South will finish a trick short. Three strikes, you are out!

Deal 19. Sneaky, Sneaky Part One

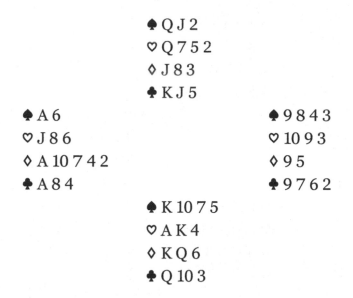

♠ Q J 2
♡ Q 7 5 2
◊ J 8 3
♣ K J 5

♠ A 6   ♠ 9 8 4 3
♡ J 8 6   ♡ 10 9 3
◊ A 10 7 4 2   ◊ 9 5
♣ A 8 4   ♣ 9 7 6 2

♠ K 10 7 5
♡ A K 4
◊ K Q 6
♣ Q 10 3

South opened 1NT and North bid 3NT. West led the ◊4

Declarer won and played a spade. West won the ace, cashed the ◊A and played another diamond. Staying off clubs where West might have an entry to his good diamonds, declarer tried for 3-3 hearts.

Making 3NT- four hearts, three spades, and two diamonds.

Routine or could the defense have prevailed?

It depends. When I played the deal, I led the ◊2. Declarer of course asked partner "Fourth best?" Partner answered correctly, "Normally yes." Assuming diamonds were 4-3, play started the same but thinking diamonds were 4-3, it seemed safe to knock out the club ace.

If he tested hearts and they were a more likely 4-2, he would be setting up extra tricks for the defense.

Declarer led a club. Down one. When partner is unlikely to be involved, seriously consider falsecarding at Trick 1.

Deal 20. Sneaky, Sneaky Part Two

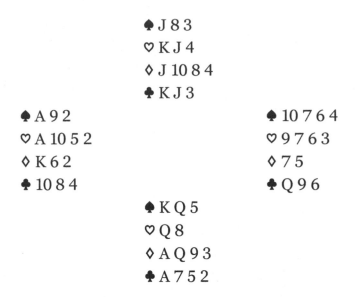

♠ J 8 3
♡ K J 4
◊ J 10 8 4
♣ K J 3

♠ A 9 2
♡ A 10 5 2
◊ K 6 2
♣ 10 8 4

♠ 10 7 6 4
♡ 9 7 6 3
◊ 7 5
♣ Q 9 6

♠ K Q 5
♡ Q 8
◊ A Q 9 3
♣ A 7 5 2

South arrives in 3NT after a 1NT – 3NT auction. West leads the ♡ 5.

Declarer wins and takes a losing diamond finesse. West plays the ♡A and clears the heart suit with the ♡2.

Declarer had planned on taking two spades, two hearts, three diamonds and two clubs. But if West had a five-card heart suit, he needed a different plan.

Upon seeing the ♡2 at Trick 4, he read West for a five-card heart suit and so was reluctant to play a spade. Instead, he tried for two hearts, three diamonds, and four clubs. He took a club finesse, losing to East. East returned a spade.

Declarer lost one club, one diamond, one spade and two hearts.

"Another one of your supposed fourth best leads, Jim?" asked declarer sarcastically.

Deal 21. Sneaky, Sneaky Part Three

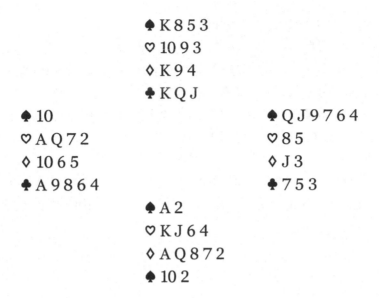

```
              ♠ K 8 5 3
              ♡ 10 9 3
              ◊ K 9 4
              ♣ K Q J
♠ 10                        ♠ Q J 9 7 6 4
♡ A Q 7 2                   ♡ 8 5
◊ 10 6 5                    ◊ J 3
♣ A 9 8 6 4                 ♣ 7 5 3
              ♠ A 2
              ♡ K J 6 4
              ◊ A Q 8 7 2
              ♣ 10 2
```

South opened 1◊ and rebid 1NT after North's response of 1♠. North raised to 3NT. West led the ♣ 4.

Declarer tested hearts by passing the ♡10 from dummy. West won the ACE. West continued with the ♣A and the ♣8.

Declarer repeated the heart finesse, passing the ♡9. West won the queen and cashed two more club tricks.

Down one losing three clubs and two hearts.

Explain that to your teammates. Tell them you had a diamond mixed in with your hearts. Or you only had four fingers on each hand and couldn't count to nine?

Deal 22. Do You See It?

	South	North	
♠ K 3			
♡ 10 6 4 2	2♣	2◇*	* Waiting
◇ Q 10 8 7 5	3♡*	3♠^	* Sets trump ^ Cue bid
♣ J 10	4NT	5♣	
	5NT	6◇^	^ Diamond king, no other king
	6♡	All Pass	

What are your choices? A passive trump? A passive club jack? A diamond?

A spade seems dangerous although the king could be right? What's it going to be, Alfie? Decide before you go on.

The whole deal:

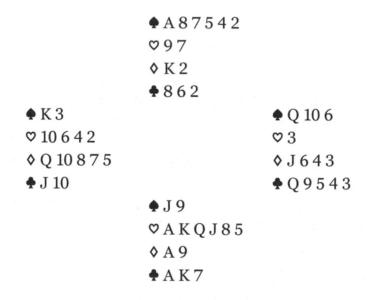

Declarer will win the opening lead and to set up the second suit, the spades, will draw trumps, then duck the first round of spades. This gives him the timing, with the suit 3-2, to draw trumps and set up the suit.

So what was the winning lead? Do you see it? The best defense is typically entry removal. A diamond lead does the job because the defenders will knock out the diamond king before the spades can be set up.

How can you tell to lead a diamond? When you have trump length, it's usually right to lead from length yourself.

Deal 23. Isn't it Obvious?

♠ 9 8 4	East	South	West	North
♡ K J 9	1◇	2♠^	3◇	4♠
◇ Q 7 6		All Pass		
♣ Q 9 7 2		^ Weak Jump Overcall		

What is your opening lead?

West led the ◇ 6. East won and returned a trump. Declarer won in hand and led a heart. West won the king to play another trump. South won in dummy, ruffed a heart, ruffed a diamond, ruffed a heart and drew trumps.

He led a club to dummy, ruffed another heart and returned to dummy with a high club to cash the good last heart for a tenth trick.

How could the defense have prevailed? Why?

West has eight HCP with strength in hearts and clubs and partner opened the bidding. What have North-South bid game on? Their good looks? Surely a distributional fit that will require what?

Yes, ruffing tricks. Put that trump on the table at Trick 1. And then again as often as possible. The contract will fail.

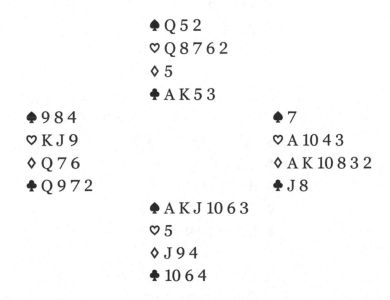

```
                      ♠ Q 5 2
                      ♡ Q 8 7 6 2
                      ◇ 5
                      ♣ A K 5 3
        ♠ 9 8 4                      ♠ 7
        ♡ K J 9                      ♡ A 10 4 3
        ◇ Q 7 6                      ◇ A K 10 8 3 2
        ♣ Q 9 7 2                    ♣ J 8
                      ♠ A K J 10 6 3
                      ♡ 5
                      ◇ J 9 4
                      ♣ 10 6 4
```

Deal 24. Now is the Time

```
♠ J 10 9         South      West      North      East
♡ A J 9          3NT                  All Pass
◊ A 8 7 2
♣ 6 4 2          Opening Lead: ♠ Jack
```

West led a passive ♠J against South's Gambling 3NT, usually a solid minor suit with very little else. Do you agree?

Declarer won the ♠Q and promptly cashed three spades and seven clubs.

Painful. What did you lead?

This is one of those auctions you should lead an ace, even if unsupported (yes, I know) to get a look. With an AK, lead the king. This is exactly what often happens. Dummy will be providing some tricks, while you have your tricks. After the ♡A, a switch to a low diamond means declarer is down one.

Lots of tricks on this deal. Remember we talked about deals with fifteen or more tricks.

```
                        North
                        ♠ A K 8 5
                        ♡ K Q 7 5
                        ◊ Q 6 4
                        ♣ J 3           East
                                        ♠ 7 6 4 2
                                        ♡ 8 6 4 3 2
                                        ◊ K J 9
                        South           ♣ 5
                        ♠ Q 3
                        ♡ 10
                        ◊ 10 5 3
                        ♣ A K Q 10 9 8 7
```

Deal 25. I'm Not Ready For That Yet

	South	West	North	East
	2♣	P	2♠^	P
	3♡	P	3♠	P
West	4NT	P	5♣	P
♠ K 4	6♡	All Pass		
♡ 10 8 5 2		^ Natural, good suit		
◇ J 10				
♣ Q 10 9 5 4	Choose your opening lead.			

West thought ◇J or ♣10. Both seemed passive, the ◇J perhaps safer. But often a more aggressive lead is suggested against a small slam. He chose the ◇J.

Declarer won the opening lead and drew trumps which were 4-1, then ducked a spade. He won the diamond continuation and played a spade to the ace and ruffed a spade. With spades a friendly 3-2 and the club entry, he claimed.

Lucky and well played? Could the defense have prevailed?

Yes, an aggressive opening lead is often a success. The bidding certainly suggested a source of tricks in dummy. What's one defense against a second suit? Remove the entry. A West listening more carefully to the bidding led the ♠K.

Sorry, Mr. South. Down one

	North ♠ A 8 7 5 3 2	
	♡ 9 7	East
A club opening lead and club	◇ 9 8 7	♠ Q 10 6
continuation also would have	♣ K 8	♡ 3
succeeded in removing an entry.		◇ Q 6 5 4 3
	South ♠ J 9	♣ J 7 6 3
South was not ready to set up the	♡ A K Q J 6 4	
spades. If declarer ducked and won the	◇ A K 2	
continuation, he could not ruff a spade	♣ A 2	

without West getting a trump promotion. If he won and drew trumps, he was an entry short of setting up the spades since trumps were 4-1.

PART THREE

AGGRESSIVE
OR
PASSIVE
DEAL
PROBLEMS

AFTER THE OPENING LEAD

OK, now what? What do expert defenders think about after the opening lead and down comes the dummy? One thought might be "Can I take my lead back?" But assuming you aren't playing against a relative, you have to live with it.

Bridge is a partnership game so both defenders should be thinking the following. Study the dummy and ask yourself – "What will declarer do with his losers?" Review the bidding. What's known about the suit led based on the opening lead?

The dummy is the key to deciding active versus passive defense. Eddie Kantar used to think LSD (Long suit? Short suit? Dead dummy?). Jerry Helms stresses BOP (Bidding, Opening Lead, Points). Marty Bergen is often quoted as saying "I never met a five card suit I didn't like." Is this a second suit hand?

What are some possible answers that will guide you to the proper defense? If declarer has winners in the dummy and will be able to discard on them, an active defense will be necessary. You will need to get your tricks before they go away. Better try to be aggressive. If there is an abundance of trumps in the dummy, dummy's losers may be going away on a second suit in declarer's hand.

If dummy has a short suit, two or fewer, declarer may be able to ruff losers in the dummy and an active defense, leading trumps, may be necessary.

If dummy looks flat with nothing special, a passive defense may be right. If declarer has losers in his hand, just let him lose them. Probably the biggest mistake defenders make is starting a new suit. Try really hard to avoid breaking a new suit for declarer that he will have to start for himself.

If dummy has two suits of four cards or longer and you feel you must attack one of them, it's usually best to attack the one that is weakest. It's almost never right to attack strong tenaces in dummy like AQJx, AJ10x, or KQ109.

Deal 26. This Can Go On Forever

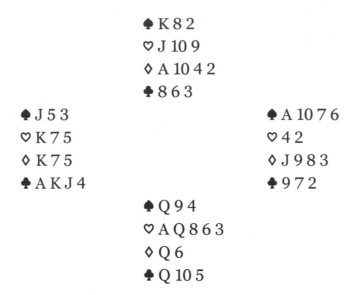

♠ K 8 2
♥ J 10 9
♦ A 10 4 2
♣ 8 6 3

♠ J 5 3
♥ K 7 5
♦ K 7 5
♣ A K J 4

♠ A 10 7 6
♥ 4 2
♦ J 9 8 3
♣ 9 7 2

♠ Q 9 4
♥ A Q 8 6 3
♦ Q 6
♣ Q 10 5

South opened 1♥ and North bid 2♥. Everyone passed. Should East-West have competed? No, balanced hands defend, suits and shape compete.

West led the ♣ ace. East played a discouraging ♣2. Now what?

With no obvious play, perhaps it's best to do nothing. Knowing when to be active or passive is not always easy to do. If you are wrong, it usually costs one or more tricks. The winning defense often is to let declarer do all the work.

The only safe continuation West has is a heart. The ♥7 is best. Declarer wins in dummy and will repeat a trump finesse to West's ♥K. Now what? Same old, same old. It's still dangerous to do anything. West exits his last heart.

Declarer leads a small diamond towards his hand. This trick goes to East's eight, declarer's queen, and West's king. Now what (again)?

East must have the ♦J or declarer would have taken a finesse. Stay passive and exit a diamond. This can go on forever. Declarer can finesse the diamond, losing to East's ♦J. East returns a diamond and declarer is down a bunch. If declarer goes up with the ♦A, it's a little better, down only two.

Boring? Not at all. Good defense doesn't have to be a thrill every moment.

Deal 27. One Strike is Not a Strike-Out

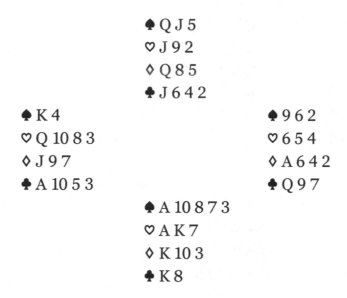

```
                    ♠ Q J 5
                    ♡ J 9 2
                    ◇ Q 8 5
                    ♣ J 6 4 2
     ♠ K 4                        ♠ 9 6 2
     ♡ Q 10 8 3                   ♡ 6 5 4
     ◇ J 9 7                      ◇ A 6 4 2
     ♣ A 10 5 3                   ♣ Q 9 7
                    ♠ A 10 8 7 3
                    ♡ A K 7
                    ◇ K 10 3
                    ♣ K 8
```

South reaches 4♠ on a 1♠ - 2♠ - 4♠ auction. What should West lead? West has a difficult lead problem but finally West leads the ♡ 3.

At Trick 1, declarer played the jack from dummy, winning the trick. (You could almost feel West's angina). At Trick 2, declarer loses a spade finesse to West.

How should West continue?

Often, the defense can survive one misstep but not two. If West is berating himself over the opening lead and panics, flailing away looking for the perfect defense, he may give away the contract. West must not break either minor suit.

There is no reason to get busy yet. If West stays passive, returning a heart or a trump, declarer will have to play the minor suits himself. If the defenders are careful, declarer may lose two clubs and possibly two diamonds.

The opening lead was a strike, not a strike-out. The defense is still at bat.

Deal 28. Patience is a Virtue

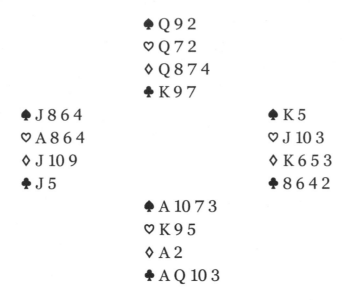

♠ Q 9 2
♡ Q 7 2
◊ Q 8 7 4
♣ K 9 7

♠ J 8 6 4
♡ A 8 6 4
◊ J 10 9
♣ J 5

♠ K 5
♡ J 10 3
◊ K 6 5 3
♣ 8 6 4 2

♠ A 10 7 3
♡ K 9 5
◊ A 2
♣ A Q 10 3

South reaches 3NT after a 1 − 2 − 3 auction. West leads the ◊ J.

At Trick 1, declarer plays the ◊Q, East covers with the ◊K and declarer wins the ◊A. Declarer leads a spade to dummy's nine, East wins the king. What should East return?

A spade. Why? It's more that East didn't want to return anything else. With the dummy flat, staying passive is best. There is no threat of a long suit.

A diamond return now would allow West to cash two diamond tricks but would set up dummy's eight of diamonds. Diamonds can wait.

Declarer won the spade return in dummy and cashed the spade ace. When spades turned out to be 4-2, declarer had too much work. By staying passive, the defense comes out on top. An aggressive lead or switch would have only helped declarer.

When declarer leads a heart, West has four winners to cash.

Deal 29. Silence in the Room

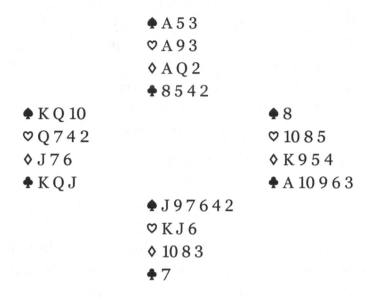

```
                    ♠ A 5 3
                    ♡ A 9 3
                    ◊ A Q 2
                    ♣ 8 5 4 2
    ♠ K Q 10                         ♠ 8
    ♡ Q 7 4 2                        ♡ 10 8 5
    ◊ J 7 6                          ◊ K 9 5 4
    ♣ K Q J                          ♣ A 10 9 6 3
                    ♠ J 9 7 6 4 2
                    ♡ K J 6
                    ◊ 10 8 3
                    ♣ 7
```

North opened 1♣ and rebid 1NT after South bid 1♠. South rebid 2♠.
West led the ♣ King.

What should the defenders be thinking upon seeing the dummy? Are there any menacing features? Is there the threat of a second suit? Are there any ruffing values in the dummy? No, no, and no.

This means the defenders need to stay as quiet as possible. Like the physician's Hippocratic oath, "First, Do No Harm."

Declarer ruffs the second club and plays the ♠A and another spade. West wins the ♠Q, cashes the ♠K, and plays......another quiet club.
Declarer ruffs and plays a heart to dummy's ace. He plays a second heart to his jack and West's queen. What should West play next?

Another quiet club. Oh wait, he doesn't have any? OK, next best is return a heart, the suit already played. Anything but starting the.......diamonds.

Declarer wins and he plays a diamond to dummy's queen. East wins but he has a club to exit. This quiet defense means declarer is going down one. If the defense ever started the diamond suit, declarer was making two spades.

Deal 30. On Second Thought

♠ K 10 6   South   West   North   East
♡ Q J   2♠   Dbl   4♠   All Pass
♦ A Q J 3 2
♣ Q J 4   Opening Lead: ♡ A

West
♠ 3 2
♡ A K 10 9   North brushes aside West's double and jumps to game.
♦ K 10 9   East plays the ♡4 at Trick 1.
♣ A 10 3 2

How should West continue the defense?

West cashed the ♡ K and shifted to a trump. Declarer won in hand and took a diamond finesse. He drew the remaining trumps and repeated the diamond finesse.

When he cashed the ♦A, West's king fell. Declarer discarded his two club losers on the diamonds.

Painful. What should West have played at Trick 3 instead of a trump?

This hand has a threat and West can see it coming. Dummy's diamonds will provide all the tricks declarer needs after drawing trumps. The diamond finesse will be working for declarer. Cash out time has come early, after Trick 2.

The only hope is East might have the ♣K. West should lay down the ♣A. When East follows with the ♣9, West will know to cash the first four tricks.

East
♠ 5 4
♡ 8 7 6 5 4
♦ 5 4
♣ K 9 8 7

South
♠ A Q J 9 8 7
♡ 3 2
♦ 8 7 6
♣ 6 5

Deal 31. Make a Decision

East	South	West	North	♠ Q 8 3
2♠	3♡	P	4♡	♡ K Q 10
All Pass				◊ A Q 10 6 5
				♣ 5 4

Opening Lead: ♠ 9

East won Trick 1 with the ♠10 and cashed
the ♠A as both West and South followed.
How should East continue?

♠ A K J 10 7 6
♡ 5 4
◊ 7 4
♣ 10 7 3

(East hand, right column)

Another high spade (passive) and hope West can overruff declarer or shift to a
club (active)?

Those diamonds in dummy looked threatening. East played another spade.
What was the result?

Since South overcalled at the three-level missing the king, queen, and ten of hearts,
his suit rates to be strong enough to ruff the third spade high.

Yes, one tries not to break a new suit but leading from ♣1073 with ♣54 in dummy
can't cost. Take your tricks.

West
♠ 9 5
♡ 3
◊ 9 8 3 2
♣ A Q J 8 6 2

South
♠ 4 2
♡ A J 9 8 7 6 2
◊ K J
♣ K 9

Deal 32. Switch or Continue?

```
           ♠ 2            East     South    West      North
           ♡ 9 4 3 2      1♡       3♠       All Pass
           ◊ K 7 6 3
West       ♣ Q 10 9 5     Opening Lead: ♡ A
♠ 8 7
♡ A 7 5
◊ Q 5 4 2      West didn't quite have enough to bid 4♡. He led the ♡A,
♣ K 6 4 3   a lead usually to be avoided without the king but certainly
            reasonable on this deal. Declarer followed with the ♡10 as
            partner played the ♡8. Declarer obviously had a singleton and
            East had played a low heart. Should West switch to a club?
```

Attitude takes priority, but reading East's card as suit preference, West shifted to a club. Declarer won in hand with the ♣J, then played the ♠A and another spade. East won the ♠K and played back a club. Declarer won the ♣A and started the diamonds, losing two diamonds but then claimed, losing one spade, one heart, and two diamonds.

How would you have continued as West at Trick 2?

There can't be any reason to get busy. A classic example of break a suit – lose a trick. Just keep those hearts coming, a passive defense. If declarer has to start both the clubs and diamonds, he loses one spade, one heart, two diamonds, and one club.
Maybe East could have played a higher heart at Trick 1?
Down one.

```
                                             East
                                             ♠ K 5
                                             ♡ K Q J 8 6
                                             ◊ A 10 9
                               South          ♣ 8 7 2
                               ♠ A Q J 10 9 6 4 3
                               ♡ 10
                               ◊ J 8
                               ♣ A J
```

Deal 33. A Switch in Time

♠ K J 9 6	South	West	North	East
♡ J 10 8	1♠	2♣^	3♡*	P
◊ 2	4♠	All Pass		
♣ K J 9 5 4	^ Hearts & a minor * Limit or better in spades			

♠ 3
♡ A K Q 6 4
◊ K J 9 5 4   West led the ♡K, showing the ♡Q, then completed her
♣ 7 2   story with the ♡A. East followed with the ♡2, then ♡3.

Opening Lead: ♡ K

Now what?

West continued passively with the ♡Q. Declarer ruffed and unblocked the ♣A. Then he led a diamond from his hand. The defense won and switched to a trump. Too late! Declarer scored three diamond ruffs, five trumps in hand, and two clubs.
Ten tricks, making four spades.

West might suspect declarer will need to ruff diamonds. Where are his HCP?

West is starring at the ◊KJ954. After cashing two heart tricks, she need switch to a trump. Reasons to lead trumps are to exit safely or to decrease declarer's ruffs.

When declarer leads a diamond, East can win and play a second trump. Declarer only has nine tricks.
Down one.

East ♠ 8 4 2
♡ 9 3 2
◊ A 7
♣ Q 10 8 6 3

South
♠ A Q 10 7 5
♡ 7 5
◊ Q 10 8 6 3
♣ A

Deal 34. Continue or Switch?

	♠ 9 5 4	South	West	North	East
	♡ J 8 6	1♡	1♠	2♣	P
	◇ Q 7	2♡	P	4♡	All Pass
	♣ A K Q 10 4				

West

♠ A K 10 6 3

♡ 9 5 2

◇ K 8 2

♣ 9 7

Opening Lead: ♠ A

Playing A from AKx, West led the ♠AK. East played the deuce then the seven as the declarer followed with the ♠QJ.

How should West continue the defense?

West continued with a passive ♠10. Declarer ruffed and cashed the ♡AK. He then cashed the ♣AK and ruffed a club with the ♡Q.

Declarer played a heart to the jack, drawing the last trump. He discarded two diamond losers on the clubs in dummy, making his contract.

How should West have defended?

If declarer had the ◇A, the contract was cold. West must shift to the ◇2 at Trick 3.

East

♠ 8 7 2

♡ 3

◇ A 10 9 4 3

♣ J 5 3 2

South

♠ Q J

♡ A K Q 10 7 4

◇ J 6 5

♣ 8 6

Deal 35. Whose Side Are You On?

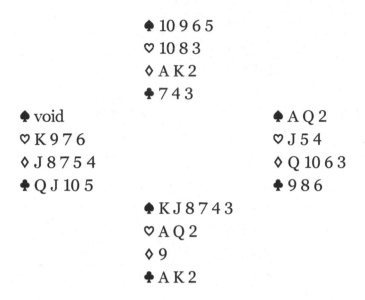

♠ 10 9 6 5
♡ 10 8 3
◊ A K 2
♣ 7 4 3

♠ void
♡ K 9 7 6
◊ J 8 7 5 4
♣ Q J 10 5

♠ A Q 2
♡ J 5 4
◊ Q 10 6 3
♣ 9 8 6

♠ K J 8 7 4 3
♡ A Q 2
◊ 9
♣ A K 2

North-South reach 4♠ after a routine 1 – 2 – 4 auction.
West leads the ♣ Q.

Declarer won in hand and went to dummy with a diamond. He discarded his club loser on the ◊K and led the ♠10. How should East continue?

East did well to win the ace. It was unlikely West had a singleton spade king or jack. East switched to the ♡4. Declarer played low and West won the ♡K.

Declarer ruffed the diamond return and cashed the ♠K. After conceding a trump to the queen, he claimed.

Making four spades.

West said, "You are supposed to be helping me, not your cousin the declarer." Was West correct?

For sure. If East stays passive and keeps his fingers off the heart suit, declarer must lose two heart tricks. After conceding a trump, declarer can reach dummy in trumps, but no matter how he starts the hearts, he loses two heart tricks.

Down one

Deal 36. But You Bid Them

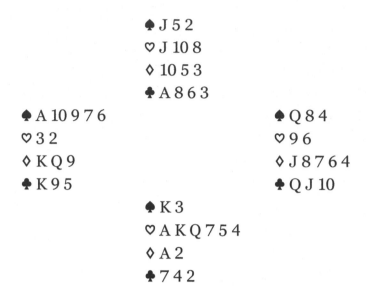

♠ J 5 2
♡ J 10 8
◊ 10 5 3
♣ A 8 6 3

♠ A 10 9 7 6
♡ 3 2
◊ K Q 9
♣ K 9 5

♠ Q 8 4
♡ 9 6
◊ J 8 7 6 4
♣ Q J 10

♠ K 3
♡ A K Q 7 5 4
◊ A 2
♣ 7 4 2

West opened 1♠ and East bid 2♠. South bid 3♡ and everyone passed. West led the ◊ K.

Declarer ducked the opening lead and won the ◊Q continuation. Declarer played two rounds of trumps ending in dummy and led a low club. East won the ♣10 and shifted to the ♠4, West's suit.

Declarer played low and West won the ♠A. Declarer made three hearts, losing one spade, one diamond, and two clubs.

"Why are you breaking the spade suit?" asked West. "You bid spades," answered East. "I though you wanted me to play your suit."

Too busy. West can't have the ♠AK or he would have led an honor. It's the same old story; whoever breaks the suit regrets it.

East can return a passive diamond. At some point, declarer has to tackle spades himself and must lose two spade tricks. Down one.

Deal 37. Boring

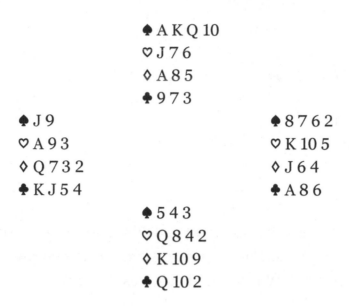

♠ A K Q 10
♡ J 7 6
◊ A 8 5
♣ 9 7 3

♠ J 9
♡ A 9 3
◊ Q 7 3 2
♣ K J 5 4

♠ 8 7 6 2
♡ K 10 5
◊ J 6 4
♣ A 8 6

♠ 5 4 3
♡ Q 8 4 2
◊ K 10 9
♣ Q 10 2

North opened 1◊ and South bid 1♡. North rebid 1♠ and South bid 1NT, ending the auction. West led the ♣ 4.

East won the ♣A and returned a club. After taking four club tricks, West had to find an exit card. He chose a low diamond. Declarer played low and captured East's ◊J with the ◊K. Declarer now has a diamond finesse position against West's queen. He won four spades and three diamond tricks, making 1NT.

Too busy? How could West have avoided this?

Render unto Caesar what is Caesar's. Defending against two balanced hands and limited HCP, it's usually best to be as passive as possible. West should exit a passive spade. Declarer has four spade and two diamond winners coming.

But both the heart and diamond suits are frozen. If declarer has to break the heart suit and/or the diamond suit, he cannot find a seventh trick.

Mike Lawrence asks how many tricks do you think it costs the defense when they switch suits at the wrong time? Experience suggests at least one, maybe more. He cautions do not be a busy defender without cause.

Don't get busy unless you know it's necessary, a lesson players hate. It's boring leading suits that don't take tricks. Feel free to wait, suggests Mike. Good advice.

Deal 38. Timing

South	West	North	East
1♠	P	2◊^	P
2♠	P	3♠	P
4♠		All Pass	

♠ A J 6
♡ A J 3
◊ K J 10 9 5
♣ 3 2

^ Game forcing
Opening Lead: ♣ 9

East
♠ 8 7
♡ K 10 9 2
◊ Q 7 4
♣ Q J 10 6

Declarer won the opening lead with the ♣A and drew two rounds of trumps ending in his hand. Then he led a diamond to the jack, losing to East's queen.

How should East continue? Which club should East return?

East returned the ♣Q. Declarer won the ♣K and led another diamond. West won the ◊A and shifted to a heart. Declarer won the ♡A and discarded two heart losers on dummy's good diamonds. Making four spades plus an overtrick.

Whoops, what went wrong? Don't tell me you fell for my tricky question?

Any club return at Trick 5 is wrong. West is unlikely to have the ♣K when she leads the ♣9. Starring at dummy's diamonds, East needs to think "It's an emergency". As the Mamas and the Papas sang "It can't wait….". A heart switch is necessary, hoping West has the ♡Q.

Could it cost a trick if South has the ♡Q?

No – South has five or six spade tricks and will soon have three diamonds. Along with two clubs and one heart, that's at least eleven. But by switching to a heart now, the defense can score two hearts and two diamonds. Down one.

West
♠ 5 3
♡ Q 6 5
◊ A 6 2
♣ 9 8 7 5 4

South
♠ K Q 10 9 4 2
♡ 8 7 4
◊ 8 3
♣ A K

64

Deal 39. Go For It

	♠ Q 10 7	South	West	North	East
	♡ K Q J 10	1♠	Dbl	Redb	P
	◊ Q J 7 2	P	2♣	2♠	P
West	♣ 8 2	3♠	P	4♠	All Pass
♠ 9 4					
♡ A 8 4 3		Opening Lead: ◊ A			
◊ A K 10					
♣ K 10 6 4					

West won Trick 1 and counted his tricks. One heart and probably two diamonds, and perhaps the club king. He cashed the other high diamond, the heart ace and exited a heart.

Unfortunately, he is still sitting with the club king as you read this, waiting for declarer to take a club finesse.

How would you have counted your tricks and defended?

Declarer is not taking any finesses. After those three high cards are gone, he has more winners in dummy than he needs.

To get a club trick, West needs to hope partner has the club queen. A club switch while he still has the ♡A is West's only hope to score the ♣K, the setting trick.

		East
		♠ 8 3
		♡ 9 7 5 2
	South	◊ 8 5 4
	♠ A K J 6 5 2	♣ Q 9 5 3
	♡ 6	
	◊ 9 6 3	
	♣ A J 7	

Is there any danger in this play? No; even if South had the ♣AQ, West was never getting the ♣K anyhow.

65

Deal 40. Don't Panic

```
              ♠ 10 8 6
              ♡ A 9 6
              ♢ K Q 2      South    West    North    East
West          ♣ 9 7 3 2    1♠       2♢      2♠       P
♠ 7 5                      4♠       All Pass
♡ K Q 5
♢ A 10 9 6 4 3            Opening Lead: ♡ K
♣ A Q
```

The KQx lead of an unbid suit is a strong lead. While it does fail on occasion, in the long run it's a big winner. Declarer ducks Trick 1, East playing the ♡J and wins the continuation. Declarer cashes the ♠AK, East following twice, and leads the ♢7.

How should West continue? Win or duck and why? If win, then what?

West won the ♢A as East played the ♢2. Was this correct? If yes, now what?

Yes. That set up two diamond tricks for declarer. It's often right to duck in these situations. East cashed the ♣A. Was this correct?

Whoops. West wasn't counting declarer's tricks. One heart, six spades and two diamonds. If declarer needs a club trick, he can't get one if you stay passive. West should return a diamond and sit back and wait.

Sometime today, declarer is going to lead a club towards his hand. Down one.

South's hand: ♠ A K Q J 9 3   ♡ 4 2   ♢ 7   ♣ K J 10 8

NB: For those who didn't like leading from the KQx, without a heart lead, declarer would have set up the diamonds and discarded his heart loser.

He would lose two clubs and a diamond but no hearts.

Deal 41. Are You Watching?

```
            ♠ Q 4 2
            ♡ Q J 9 5      South    West    North    East
            ◊ Q J          1♠       P       1NT      P
West        ♣ K 10 7 4     2♠       P       4♠       All Pass
♠ 7 5
♡ 10 6 4 2                 Opening Lead: ♡ 2
◊ A 9 8 7
♣ J 5 2
```

Trick 1 proceeds ♡2; 5; A; K. East returns the ◊10.
Declarer plays low. How should West continue the defense?

West, not anxious to break the club suit, having read about all the bad things that befall players who break new suits, returned a diamond. Declarer won and drew trumps. He discarded two club losers on the good hearts in dummy.

Making four spades with an overtrick.

East moaned, "Didn't you see the good hearts? I led a high diamond."

Yes, breaking new suits is usually wrong unless it's right. To break a new suit is a "Desperado Play." East's high diamond could not tell West what suit to lead, but it did say what suit not to lead. If East wanted a diamond return, he would have led a low diamond at Trick 2.

With the hearts in dummy ready to go, an active defense is needed. West should lead a club at Trick 3 and hope for the best.

Success! East scores two club tricks. Down one.

```
                              East
                              ♠ J 3
                              ♡ A 8 7 3
              South           ◊ 10 5 2
              ♠ A K 10 9 8 6  ♣ A Q 9 6
              ♡ K
              ◊ K 6 4 3
              ♣ 8 3
```

Deal 42. Active Yes, But Then?

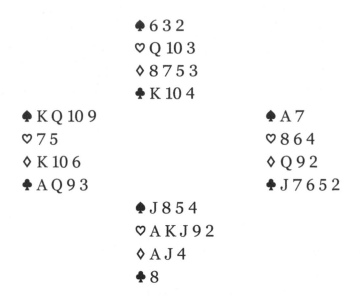

♠ 6 3 2
♡ Q 10 3
◊ 8 7 5 3
♣ K 10 4

♠ K Q 10 9   ♠ A 7
♡ 7 5   ♡ 8 6 4
◊ K 10 6   ◊ Q 9 2
♣ A Q 9 3   ♣ J 7 6 5 2

♠ J 8 5 4
♡ A K J 9 2
◊ A J 4
♣ 8

South opened 1♡ and West made a take-out double. North bid 2♡ and everyone passed. Should West have doubled again? West led the ♠ K.

Declarer played low and East smartly overtook to unblock the suit. East returned his last spade. West cashed a third spade and led his last spade. Declarer ruffed high and led a trump to his hand to lead a club. West won the ♣A.

Declarer had a trump entry in dummy to reach the ♣K. He discarded one diamond loser. Five hearts in hand, one ruff in dummy, one club and one diamond.
Eight tricks, making two hearts.

A very poor result for East-West who likely can make 3♣, but 2♡ should go down. Place the blame.

East was right to be active in overtaking but since he could not overruff dummy, there was no point returning a spade. A diamond shift at Trick 2 will set up two diamond tricks before the club ace is played.
Or East could simply duck, win Trick 2 and shift to achieve the same result.

The defense will score three spades, two diamonds and one club. Down one.

68

Deal 43. Even More Boring

West	North	East	South
1♡	Dbl	P	2♠
3♡	4♠	All Pass	

♠ K Q J 10
♡ Q J
◊ 7 5 3
♣ A K Q J

East
♠ 6 4 3
♡ 4
◊ 9 6 4 2
♣ 9 6 5 4 2

Opening Lead: ♡ Ace

West continues the ♡K.

What should East discard at Trick 2?

How should the defense proceed?

East, trying not to yawn with his not-very-exciting hand discarded a deuce.

Declarer ruffed the third heart, drew trumps, and discarded his remaining losers on dummy's clubs.

What should East have discarded?

A three, not a two. What, you say, he doesn't have a three to discard?

What about the three of spades?

West opened the bidding. Where are his HCP? In diamonds and the defense had better grab those tricks quickly.

At Trick 2, East should ruff partner's ♡K and shift to the ◊6.

Down one.

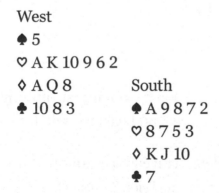

West
♠ 5
♡ A K 10 9 6 2
◊ A Q 8
♣ 10 8 3

South
♠ A 9 8 7 2
♡ 8 7 5 3
◊ K J 10
♣ 7

It just shows you never know when it's your turn to shine. Who needs HCP?

Deal 44. What's His Card Mean?

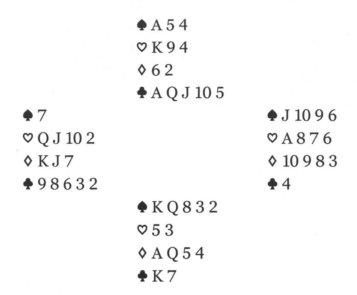

♠ A 5 4
♥ K 9 4
♦ 6 2
♣ A Q J 10 5

♠ 7   ♠ J 10 9 6
♥ Q J 10 2   ♥ A 8 7 6
♦ K J 7   ♦ 10 9 8 3
♣ 9 8 6 3 2   ♣ 4

♠ K Q 8 3 2
♥ 5 3
♦ A Q 5 4
♣ K 7

South opened 1♠ and North bid 2♣, game forcing. South bid 2♦ and North bid 2♠. South bid 3♣ and North bid 4♠. West led the ♥ Q.

Notice on a good day, 3-2 trumps and the heart ace on-side, twelve tricks.

Declarer ducked Trick 1, East playing the ♥8, and ducked the heart continuation. Declarer ruffed the third heart and played the ♠KQ. When West discarded, South started the clubs, East ruffed the second club and led a diamond.

Declarer won the ♦A, drew the last trump with the ♠A and ran the remaining clubs pitching his diamonds. Making four spades.

Asses the blame for this mishap?

Both East and West contributed, mostly East. Looking at dummy's good clubs, instead of sitting by, he should overtake the second heart to switch to a diamond.

When in with his trump trick, the defense can cash a diamond trick for down one. West could have helped by switching to the ♥2 at Trick 2. Since West holds Trick 1, the attitude is known. East's ♥8 should be a count signal so West can lead the ♥2 at Trick 2.

Deal 45. Stay Calm

	♠ Q 9	South	West	North	East
	♡ K 10 6 4	1♡	P	2NT^	P
	◊ A J 4	3NT#	P	6♡*	All Pass
West	♣ A 10 9 8				
♠ J 10 8 7 6 4		^ A Jacoby Forcing Raise			
♡ 9 7 3		# Balanced, extras, 15-17 HCP			
◊ K 2		* It's your lead! No more information			
♣ Q 5		Opening Lead: ♠ J			

Trick 1 consists of ♠J; Q; K, A. Declarer draws three rounds of trumps, East following once, then discards a spade and a diamond. Declarer leads the ◊Q; K; A; 2. Declarer cashes the ◊J and ruffs a diamond. He exits a spade to West's ♠10 as East follows. How should West continue?

Declarer has stripped the spades and diamonds. He started with two spades, five hearts, and two diamonds. To avoid a ruff/sluff, West broke the club suit, properly leading the ♣Q. However, declarer won the ace in dummy and successfully finessed East for the ♣J. Making six hearts.

If West is going to break the club suit, the queen is the right card. Do you agree with the defense and we should credit declarer for good technique?

No, West erred. He has to stay passive. Since he knows South is 2=5=2=4, one ruff/sluff won't help declarer. If West stays passive and return a spade, he will set six hearts.

	East
	♠ K 5 2
South	♡ 2
♠ A 3	◊ 10 9 8 7 5 3
♡ A Q J 8 5	♣ J 6 2
◊ Q 6	
♣ K 7 4 3	

If South starts the club suit, he must lose a club. If East-West start the club suit, declarer has a chance to play for no losers.

Deal 46. Anything But

South	West	North	East
1♠	P	1NT^	P
3♠	P	4♠	All Pass

^ Forcing, one round

Opening Lead: ♡ K

♠ Q J 5
♡ J 8 7 5
♦ K Q J 10
♣ J 8

East
♠ 10 6
♡ A 10 9 6
♦ A 6 5 2
♣ Q 10 9

Declarer ruffed the second heart and played the ♠A and a spade to the ♠Q, West following twice. Next declarer led the ♦K. East took the ace, West playing a high spot. How should East continue the defense? Active or passive? Why?

East, seeing the good diamonds in dummy, switched to a club. Which club? Doesn't matter. Making four spades.

What should East be doing before continuing?

Count declarer's tricks. Six hearts and three diamonds. If declarer has the ♣A, it's all over. But if he has the ♣K, East better return........anything but a club.

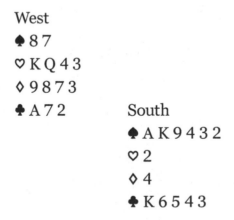

West
♠ 8 7
♡ K Q 4 3
♦ 9 8 7 3
♣ A 7 2

South
♠ A K 9 4 3 2
♡ 2
♦ 4
♣ K 6 5 4 3

If East returns anything other than a club, at some point, declarer has to play a club and cannot take a club trick. If East leads one, declarer can guess to play low.

Deal 47. Another Don't Panic

	♠ K Q 9 5	South	West	North	East
	♡ Q J 10 9 8	1♠	2♠^	4♠	4NT
	◇ Q J	5♠	All Pass		
West	♣ J 8		^ Hearts and a minor		
♠ 10					
♡ K 7 6 5 3			Opening Lead: ◇ A		
◇ A K 10 9 7					
♣ A 9					

It looks good for the defense, but declarer ruffs the opening lead. He cashes the ♠AK, East following, and ruffs the last diamond. Declarer cashes the ♡A and leads a heart to West's king.

How should West continue the defense?

West cashed the ♣A and continued a club. Declarer won the ♣K.
Making five spades.

What would have helped West make the correct play?

Again, count declarer's tricks. Six spades and four hearts. That's it, ten. Another example of "Render unto Caesar that which is Caesar's." No matter his distribution, to get an eleventh trick it will have to come from clubs.

West can just play back a heart. Let declarer go first in clubs.
Down one.

		East	♠ 6 2
			♡ 2
	South		◇ 8 6 5 4 3 2
	♠ A J 8 7 4 3		♣ Q 10 5 3
	♡ A 4		
	◇ void		
	♣ K 7 6 4 2		

Deal 48. Count or Panic

	♠ J 8 3 2	East	South	West	North
	♡ A 4	2♡	2♠	4♡	4♠
	◊ J 5		All Pass		
West	♣ Q J 10 9 7				
♠ K 7 6					
♡ Q 9 8 5			Opening Lead: ♡ 5		
◊ A 10 7 3					
♣ A 4					

Declarer won the ♡A and led a spade to his queen and West's king. Now what? Slow hand? Fast hand? West played another heart and declarer ruffed. After drawing trumps, declarer led the ♣K. West was back in.

How should West continue? Active or passive?

West cashed the ◊A and played another diamond. Declarer had ten tricks.

How many tricks does declarer have?

This is just like the previous deal. West went active when he should have continued passive. Count declarer's tricks. Five trumps and four clubs. Do you remember the song "As Time Goes By?" It's still the same old story, a fight.....

If declarer needs a diamond trick, he can only get one if the defenders go first. Just stay passive, lead back a club and he will come to you. Eventually the defense will take two diamond tricks Patience is a virtue.

Down one.

		East
		♠ 5
		♡ K J 10 7 6 2
	South	◊ Q 6 2
	♠ A Q 10 9 4	♣ 8 6 3
	♡ 3	
	◊ K 9 8 4	
	♣ K 5 2	

Deal 49. Saving An Overtrick

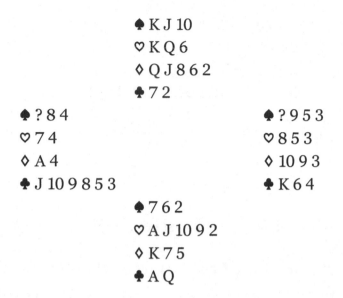

♠ K J 10
♡ K Q 6
◇ Q J 8 6 2
♣ 7 2

♠ ? 8 4
♡ 7 4
◇ A 4
♣ J 10 9 8 5 3

♠ ? 9 5 3
♡ 8 5 3
◇ 10 9 3
♣ K 6 4

♠ 7 6 2
♡ A J 10 9 2
◇ K 7 5
♣ A Q

South opened 1♡ and North bid 2◇, game forcing. South raised to 3◇.
North bid 3♡ but South signed off in 4♡. West led the ♣ J.

East played low, knowing declarer had both the ace and queen. Declarer won the
♣Q and drew trumps. He led a diamond to the dummy, then another diamond to
West's ◇A.

Not wanting to break a new suit, West exited passively with a club. Declarer ruffed
and discarded two spades on the diamonds. He conceded the last trick. Making four
hearts plus an overtrick.

Could you have saved the overtrick? Suppose you were playing matchpoints?

Perhaps. West knows declarer has five heart tricks and four diamond tricks. Since
he is known to have the club ace, that's ten tricks. If declarer has the ♠A, he might
have tried for slam. If he has the ♠Q he would have opened 1NT. Now is the time to
put him to a spade guess before he takes all his tricks.

If West's spades are ♠Qxx, almost surely East has the ♠A. If West has the ♠A, East
has the ♠Q. Put declarer to a guess now.

Deal 50. The Wooden Soldier

South	West	North	East
1◇	P	1♠	P
2♣	P	2♡^	P
2NT	P	3NT	All Pass

^ 4th Suit Forcing

Opening Lead: ♡J

♠ K Q 6 3
♡ 8 7 2
◇ Q 3 2
♣ K Q J

Evelyn - East

♠ A 10 9 8
♡ A 6 5 4
◇ 8 4
♣ 9 7 2

East won the ♡A at Trick 1. How should East continue?

Evelyn woodenly returned a heart. Declarer won, went to dummy with a club and took a losing diamond finesse. West switched to a spade, but declarer had plenty of tricks.

The expression on Jim's face told it all.

"What," asked Evelyn? "You told me to always return your suit."

True if you were a wooden soldier but a thinking bridge player would remember the auction too. South likely has nine minor suit cards and three hearts, hence a singleton spade.

At Trick 2, instead of a passive heart, East should return the ♠10. This runs to dummy's queen. When West wins the ◇K, now a spade continuation gives the defense three more tricks. Down one.

Jim - West
♠ J 7 5 2
♡ J 10 3
◇ K 6 5
♣ 8 6 4

South
♠ 4
♡ K Q 9
◇ A J 10 9 7
♣ A 10 5 3

76

Deal 51. Déjà Vu

North	East	South	West	♠ K 10 5
1◊	P	1NT	P	♡ A K Q
2NT	All Pass			◊ Q J 10 9 8 5
				♣ K

Opening Lead: ♣ J

Infamous Evelyn

♠ A J 9 8 6
♡ 10 6 4 2
◊ K
♣ 6 3 2

The ♣K in dummy won the first trick.

Declarer led a diamond from dummy. East won. How should East continue?

She returned a passive club. Declarer won the ace and led another diamond.

I won the ace and shifted to a low spade. Declarer played the ♠10 from dummy, losing to the jack, but the best the defense could do now was cash the ♠A to prevent any more overtricks.

"Evelyn," I asked, "Didn't we just have a hand like this?"

Even Evelyn should see that a passive club return to declarer's known ♣AQ is futile. One more diamond lead will set up four diamond tricks. Declarer has three club tricks and three heart tricks in the bag. The only hope is spades.

South passed 2NT. He can't have much more than the ♣AQ. A spade shift at Trick 2 to my likely ♠Q will give declarer one spade trick, but will set up our spade suit.

When I win the second diamond, the defense can cash four more spade tricks. Down one.

Jim - West
♠ Q 7 2
♡ 8 7 3
◊ A 6 3
♣ J 10 9 8

South
♠ 4 3
♡ J 9 5
◊ 7 4 2
♣ A Q 7 5 4

Deal 52. Cut Off

	♠ 9 3 2	South	West	North	East
	♡ 9 2	1♡	P	1NT	P
	◊ A Q J 4 2	3♡	All Pass		
West	♣ 8 5 2				
♠ Q 10 6 4		Opening Lead: ◊ 10			
♡ A 8					
◊ 10 9 8 7					
♣ A 10 3					

Trick 1 lost to South's king as East played the six. Declarer led the ♡K and West won the ace. Now what?

West switched to a low spade. East won the ♠A and returned a spade. Declarer won the ♠K, drew trumps and claimed: five trump tricks, one spade, and five diamonds. Eleven tricks, conceding a club at the end.

"Why didn't you bid game," asked South? East politely kept quiet.
Forget game. Was there a defense to defeat three hearts?

Perhaps. Consider the diamond position. East played the six at Trick 1.
The 5 and 3 are missing. East cannot have both. Either East is ruffing diamonds or they are 2-2. Instead of breaking new suits, a diamond return at Trick 3 cuts declarer off from the dummy.

He cannot continue diamonds since there are outstanding trumps. He may guess how to continue, he may not, but if West breaks a new suit, it's no problem- eleven tricks.

		East
		♠ A 8 5
	South	♡ 7 4 3
	♠ K J 7	◊ 6 3
	♡ K Q J 10 6 5	♣ Q J 9 6 4
	◊ K 5	
	♣ K 7	

Deal 53. Changing Trains

♠ 10 6 5	South	West	North	East
♡ J 8 7	1♡	P	1NT^	P
◇ K Q J 6	2◇	P	4♡*	All Pass
♣ A 7 2	^ Forcing, one round * Hand got better?			

♠ K J 7 4
♡ A K 5
◇ 8 5
♣ Q J 10 3

Opening Lead: ♣ Q

Declarer won in hand with the ♣K as partner played a discouraging four. Declarer led a trump and West won.

How should West continue the defense?

He continued a passive ♣10. East played the ♣9, suit preference for spades, but it was too late.

Declarer won the ♣A and played another trump. West won with his other high honor and continued full speed ahead with the ♣J. Declarer ruffed, drew the last trump and discarded one spade loser on the long diamond.

Making four hearts.

East asked West, "Did you give any thought to changing trains?"

Club continuations were not going to set this contract. The defense needed two spade tricks. If declarer had ♠AQ, he would have opened 1NT. At Trick 3, West must switch to a spade before declarer can finish the trumps. East produces the ♠Q like a good partner.

Declarer loses two spades and two hearts. Down one.

East
♠ Q 8 3
♡ 4 3
◇ 10 9 7 4
♣ 9 8 5 4

South
♠ A 9 2
♡ Q 10 9 6 2
◇ A 3 2
♣ K 6

Deal 54. The Unsuspecting Hero

South	West	North	East	
1♡	Dbl	2NT^	3♣	♠ 8 6 3 2
4♡	All Pass			♡ K 10 8 7
				♢ K 10 5
^ Limit heart raise or better				♣ A 4

East
♠ 7 5 4
♡ 5
♢ 9 7 3 2
♣ K 10 8 7 3

Opening Lead: ♣ Q

At Trick 1, declarer played low. Which card should East play? Encourage with the ♣10 or suggest a switch with the ♣3?

East played an encouraging ♣10. West continued a low club to dummy's ace. Declarer drew trumps and led a low diamond towards dummy. West won and exited a diamond. Declarer won the ♢K and ruffed his last diamond. He went to dummy and led the ♠2 spade to his ♠10. West won the ♠Q and was endplayed. Either a club, ruff/sluff or a spade into declarer's ♠AJ meant declarer was making four hearts.

Was there a line of play to defeat the contract. Anybody's fault?

100% East's. East? He didn't have anything. Really? A defender must stay awake. Just because you have a boring hand doesn't mean you may not have a crucial role. Do you see it?

The correct answer to the two questions above was neither. Forget the ♣10 or the ♣3. Overtake partner's ♣Q with your ♣K and return a spade, taking West off the endplay. Declarer goes down one.

West ♠ K Q 9
♡ 6 2
♢ A Q J 4
♣ Q J 9 5

South
♠ A J 10
♡ A Q J 9 4 3
♢ 8 6
♣ 6 2

Deal 55. Are You Awake?

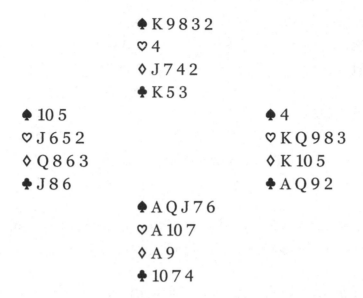

♠ K 9 8 3 2
♡ 4
◊ J 7 4 2
♣ K 5 3

♠ 10 5
♡ J 6 5 2
◊ Q 8 6 3
♣ J 8 6

♠ 4
♡ K Q 9 8 3
◊ K 10 5
♣ A Q 9 2

♠ A Q J 7 6
♡ A 10 7
◊ A 9
♣ 10 7 4

East opened 1♡, South overcalled 1♠. At favorable vulnerability, West jumped to 3♡ despite his balanced hand. North bid 4♠. West led the ♡ 2.

Declarer has a diamond loser and has to avoid losing three club tricks. Look carefully at this club suit. If declarer starts the clubs, he will likely lose three tricks. If the defenders start the suit, declarer will likely lose only two tricks.

Declarer won the opening lead and played the ◊A and another diamond. West had to duck or declarer could ruff out East's ◊K. Declarer played the ◊J from dummy. East won the ◊K and stayed passive, returning a diamond. Declarer ruffed, then ruffed a heart in dummy. He ruffed the last diamond in his hand and drew trumps.

Declarer led his last heart towards dummy apparently intending to ruff in dummy. Are you awake?

If West fails to cover with the ♡J, it's curtains for the defense. Declarer will discard a club, endplaying East. If West covers, it's curtains for the declarer.

If declarer discards, now the defense can take two clubs. If declarer ruffs, he has to start the clubs.

Were you sleeping or awake? You can tell me. I won't tell anyone.

Deal 56. One Time At Bat

South	West	North	East
1♠	2♡	2♠	3♡
4♠	All Pass		

♠ J 10 8 6
♡ J 9 2
♢ J 10 9 5
♣ A 6

Opening Lead: ♡ K

♠ 7
♡ A 8 5 4
♢ 7 3 2
♣ J 10 9 4 3

How should East defend? Encourage? Discourage?

East played an encouraging ♡8 at Trick 1. Declarer ruffed the low heart continuation and led the ♠K. West won the ♠A and exited his last high heart.

Declarer lost a diamond finesse but was able to discard his club loser on the long diamond.

Assess the blame for letting this one get away.

Like a previous few deals ago, East had one time 'at bat'. There was no future in hearts. East must overtake with the ♡A at Trick 1 and switch to the ♣J so the defense can set up a club trick before the diamonds are established.

It may not matter; perhaps West has the ♢AQ but this is your only chance if necessary.

West
♠ A
♡ K Q 10 7 3
♢ K 6 4
♣ K 7 5 2

South
♠ K Q 9 5 4 3 2
♡ 6
♢ A Q 8
♣ Q 8

Deal 57. In the Right Order

East	South	West	North	♠ A Q 10 3
1♣	P	1♡	Dbl	♡ A J
2♡	2♠	P	4♠	◇ K Q J 10 4

All Pass · · · ♣ K 5 · · · Evelyn - East

♠ 8 6 5
♡ K 6 4
◇ A 5
♣ A Q 8 7 3

Opening Lead: ♣ 10

Evelyn opened 1♣ and I bid 1♡, having learned not to pass one of a minor with a five-card major regardless of HCP strength. North-South reached 4♠. No support doubles or redoubles with Evelyn, please. I led the ♣ 10.

Evelyn won the first two club tricks, then started thinking about the deal. She played back a trump. Declarer took five trump tricks, four diamond tricks, and one club trick, the ♣J.

"Evelyn, what's the one card I can't have," I asked?

The ♣J. I led the ♣10. While a passive defense won't help, Evelyn can't cash a second club without setting up South's ♣J. Since dummy's diamonds are such a threat to a passive defense, East must switch to a heart at Trick 2.

On a good day, West has the ♡Q. If not, East probable wasn't getting a heart trick anyhow. Once the diamonds are set up, declarer will discard her heart losers.

Jim – West
♠ 9
♡ Q 10 7 3 2
◇ 8 7 6 3 2
♣ 10 4

South
♠ K J 7 4 2
♡ 9 8 5
◇ 9
♣ J 9 6 2

Deal 58. The Other Side

	♠ A 8	South	West	North	East
	♡ J 10 5	1♡	Dbl	Redbl	3♠^
	◊ K Q J 10 7	P	P	4♡	All Pass
	♣ J 10 5	^ Preemptive			

♠ K 5 3   Opening Lead: ♣ A
♡ 8 3 2
◊ A 9 3
♣ A K 7 2

West's take-out double with three small hearts was marginal.
East played a discouraging ♣4 at Trick 1.
How should West continue?

West passively switched to a trump. Declarer drew trumps and led a diamond.
West won his three tricks and declarer had the rest.

What would you have played at Trick 2?

The situation looks grim. If West cashes the ♣K, dummy's ♣J is probably good.
This is a fast hand. There is no time to be passive. Once the diamonds are good, the
defense will be finished.

At Trick 2, West must switch to a spade while he still has the ◊A. If East doesn't
have the ♠Q, the defense probably isn't getting a spade trick anyhow.

East is a good partner. The defense takes one spade, one diamond, and two clubs.
Down one.

East
♠ Q 10 7 6 4 2
♡ 6
◊ 8 4
♣ 9 8 6 4

South
♠ J 9
♡ A K Q 9 7 4
◊ 6 5 2
♣ Q 3

Deal 59. Tough One

	♠ J 10 9 5	South	West	North	East
	♡ K Q J 10	1♠	P	3♠^	P
	◊ 8 3	4♠		All Pass	
	♣ K 8 3		^ Limit raise		

♠ 6 4
♡ A 7 4
◊ K 9 6 2
♣ Q J 10 6

Opening Lead: ♣ Q

Declarer ducked Trick 1, East played the ♣9 and West continued with the ♣10. Declarer ducked again. East played the ♣2.

How should West continue?

What did the ♣9 mean? West played the ♣J. Declarer ruffed and drew trumps in two rounds. Then he led a low heart. It didn't matter when West took the ace; declarer could discard his diamond loser on the long heart in dummy.

Making four spades.

Would you have found the diamond switch before the ♡A is dislodged?

That's a scary switch. Declarer is very likely to have the ◊AQ. Would East's carding help?

This is similar to a previous deal. The attitude is known so the ♣9 should be count. West will know hopefully how to continue. Tough one.

East
♠ 7
♡ 8 5 2
◊ Q J 10 7 5
♣ A 9 5 2

South
♠ A K Q 8 3 2
♡ 9 6 3
◊ A 4
♣ 7 4

Deal 60. False Count

♠Q 9 5 3
♡2
♢Q J 10 9
♣A K 5 3

West	North	East	South
1♡	Dbl	3♡^	4♠
All Pass			

^ Preemptive

Opening Lead: ♢ Ace

♠A 2
♡Q 9 7 6 3
♢A K 6 4
♣Q 8

Trick 1 proceeded ♢9, 3, 2. How should West continue?

It looks grim. Remember what we discussed. Assume you can beat the contract, but West can add. East is broke. West switched passively to a heart.

Declarer won, knocked out the ♠A and won the heart continuation. He drew the last trump and claimed after conceding another diamond, discarding two club losers on the diamonds.

Was there any hope for the defense? Passive didn't work.

When you see a source of tricks in dummy, think 'active'. What card did West need to play East for? No aces or kings, true, but how about the ♣J? East can help by playing the ♢8 at Trick 1, the ♢3 at Trick 2.

At Trick 3, West continues with another diamond. West is at first surprised East follows. South can discard one club but when West wins the first trump, he can play a fourth diamond.

East will ruff and South will overruff. But now South can't use the good ♢Q in dummy and has to lose a club to East's ♣J.

East ♠8 7
♡J 10 8 5 4
♢8 5 3
♣J 10 2

South
♠K J 10 6 4
♡A K
♢7 2
♣9 7 6 4

Deal 61. Encourage?

West	North	East	South	♠ 10 6 5 3 2
1♡	P	1NT^	2♣	♡ 2
3♣	4♠	All Pass		◊ Q 10 5 2

^ Forcing one round

Opening Lead: ♡ K

♠ 10 6 5 3 2
♡ 2
◊ Q 10 5 2
♣ A 8 6

East
♠ 9
♡ A 10 3
◊ A J 9 6 4 3
♣ 9 7 2

How should East plan the defense at Trick 1?

He played the ♡10. Was that to encourage a continuation or suggest a shift to a diamond? Or should he play the ♡3?

West shifted to the ◊8. East won the ◊A as declarer dropped the king.

East shifted to the ♣9; Q; K; A. Declarer discarded his remaining club on dummy's ◊Q. He knocked out the ♠A.

Making four spades.

Should East-West have bid 5♡ which makes as the cards lie?

Yes (see note below) but at least defeat four spades. Forget encourage, suit preference, whatever. This deal needs active defense and in a big hurry.

East must overtake the ♡K at Trick 1 to shift to a club before, not after the ◊A is dislodged. Declarer will now lose one trick in each suit, down one.

West ♠ A
♡ K Q J 6 5
◊ 8 7   South
♣ K J 10 4 3   ♠ K Q J 8 7 4
               ♡ 9 8 7 4
               ◊ K
               ♣ Q 5

Note: East, for his 1NT forcing bid has good heart support and extra playing strength. A hand to declare, not defend. He should bid 5♡.

Deal 62. Derby Time

East	South	West	North	♠ A 8 4
1♣	1♦	Dbl^	2♦	♡ 9 6 3
2♡	3♦	All Pass		♦ Q 9 6

^ Negative double

Opening lead: ♡ Q

♠ A 8 4
♡ 9 6 3
♦ Q 9 6
♣ Q J 9 6

East
♠ 7 6
♡ A K 10 4
♦ 7 4 3
♣ A 7 4 3

West led the ♡QJ at Tricks 1 and 2, then continued with a third heart. How should East defend?

The race was on, but declarer was already ahead. He ruffed the third heart and drew trumps. Then declarer led the ♣10.

East won the ♣A and switched to the ♠7; J, Q, A. Declarer played a second club. West won the ♣K and led another spade but it was too late. Dummy's last two clubs provided a place to discard spade losers. Making three diamonds.

Could you have run a more successful race?

Yes, if you were more active at the beginning. Continuing hearts was too passive. East should overtake the heart lead at Trick 1 and get a spade on the table. Now the defense is in the lead.

The danger of the club suit is real and the defenders need defend efficiently. A more active defense at the beginning will lead to a more successful ending.

West
♠ Q 10 9 5
♡ Q J 5 2
♦ 8 5
♣ K 5 2

South
♠ K J 3 2
♡ 8 7
♦ A K J 10 2
♣ 10 8

Deal 63. If You See It, Do It

North	East	South	West	♠ K 10 7 5
1♣	1♡	1♠	4♡	♡ 5 4
4♠	All Pass			◊ A K

♣ Q J 10 9 7   Evelyn- East

Opening Lead: ♡ King

♠ 4 2
♡ A J 9 6 3
◊ Q 10 9 7 6
♣ 3

Which heart should Evelyn play at Trick 1?

She played an encouraging ♡9. I continued with a second heart. Declarer ruffed and started the trumps. I won the ♠A and later the ♣K.
Making four spades.

"Couldn't you see how to beat four spades, Evelyn?" I asked.
What was I referring to? How could we have prevailed?

Evelyn should take over at Trick 1. Overtake the ♡K with the ♡A to shift to her singleton club. It's likely I have a high club honor.

Declarer will win the ♣A and try to draw trumps quickly, but I will win the first spade, cash the ♣K and play a third club. Evelyn's club ruff is the setting trick.

Jim -West
♠ A 8
♡ K Q 10 8 2
◊ J 4
♣ K 8 6 2

South
♠ Q J 9 6 3
♡ 7
◊ 8 5 3 2
♣ A 5 4

Yes, the bidding was a bit strange. Evelyn could have overcalled 2NT, diamonds and hearts after a 1♣ opening.

Deal 64. Good Guess

East	South	West	North	♠ 9 7 4 2
1♠	4♡	All Pass		♡ J
				◊ K Q J 6 3
Opening Lead: ♠ 5				♣ K J 8

East
♠ A K 8 6 3
♡ A
◊ A 10 8 2
♣ 7 6 3

East won the opening lead. Some hands require good guessing, not just good card play. Had West led a singleton? Could continuing spades, a passive defense, be right in any case? How should East continue?

East returned a top spade but declarer ruffed. Declarer led a small heart and East won the ♡A. Declarer won the spade return, drew trumps and after giving up the ◊A took the rest. Making four hearts.

Any other ideas? You know from the opening lead the missing spades are 3-1.

If South has the singleton spade, he is likely to have some minor length. Instead of a passive spade return, East can play the ◊A at Trick 2 and continue with another diamond.

After winning the first trump trick, perhaps a third diamond lead will be fruitful? Home run! West's ♡10 is promoted to the setting trick.

West
♠ Q 10 5
♡ 10 6 4
◊ 7 5
♣ 10 9 5 4 2

South
♠ J
♡ K Q 9 8 7 5 3 2
◊ 9 4
♣ A Q

Deal 65. Mission Impossible

Evelyn

♠ 9 2
♡ K 9 6 3 2
◇ 9 8 3 2
♣ 7 5

♠ J 8 4
♡ Q 7 4
◇ A J 7
♣ K J 10 4

Jim

♠ 5 3
♡ A J 10
◇ K 10 5 4
♣ A 9 6 2

♠ A K Q 10 7 6
♡ 8 5
◇ Q 6
♣ Q 8 3

South opened 1♠ and reached 4♠ on an uncontested auction.
Evelyn led the ♡ 3.

I played the ♡10 which won Trick 1. It was tempting to play passive, just cash the
♡A, play a third heart. But declarer will ruff, draw trumps, and force out my ♣A. Any
diamond losers will go on the clubs.

To get Evelyn to lead a diamond, I led the ♡J to Evelyn's ♡K. Evelyn stopped to
think. Then beaming, she turned to declarer and said, "I think you ducked your ace
once too often. Now you will get your ace ruffed."

She continued with the ♡2. But it was my ace that got ruffed.

"Evelyn, if I wanted to play on hearts, I would have cashed the ace myself," I said,
trying to keep calm.
She countered with "Aren't you the one who keeps telling me 'Cash an ace, blow a
trick!'?

When Evelyn wins Trick 2 with the ♡K, she should do what's expected.
I think I was expecting Mission Impossible.

Deal 66. Star Trek

North	East	South	West	♠ A 6 5	
1◊	P	1♡	P	♡ 8 3	
3◊	P	3NT	All Pass	◊ A K Q J 10 6	
				♣ Q J	**East**
					♠ J 10
Opening Lead: ♠ 2					♡ Q J 6
					◊ 8 5 4 2
					♣ A 8 7 4

Declarer takes Trick 1 with dummy's ♠A and leads the ♣Q. Marvin Gaye asked, "What's Going On?" How should East defend?

On his highly recommended website BridgeClues, Mike Lawrence compared some bridge problems to the Star Trek movie and Spock trying to compute the orbit for the Klingon Bird of Prey. While being hurled into the future, he said he would have to make a good guess.

Lawrence pointed out that similarly bridge can be an obfuscating experience at times. The line of defense here is a good example. Two good players can strongly differ about the best line of play.

If East takes the ♣A, should he return a passive ♠J or an active ♡Q?

Declarer has made a strange play at Trick 1. He likely has the ♠K in hand, keeping it as an entry to his clubs. Lawrence suggests a heart switch but agrees there is no guarantee, just that it has merit and requires less than other plays.

West	♠ Q 8 4 2		
	♡ A 10 9 7		
	◊ 7 3	**South**	
	♣ 6 5 3	♠ K 9 7 3	
		♡ K 5 4 2	
		◊ 9	
		♣ K 10 9 2	

Some hands simple do not offer clear inferences, just make the best guess you can. His bridge site www.bridgeclues2.com is full of good advice. Thanks, Mike.

Deal 67. What's Her Shape?

```
              ♠ J 5        South   West    Nort        East
              ♡ K J 8 7    1♡      P       2NT^        P
              ◊ 9 4 2      3♡      P       4♣          P
West          ♣ A K 10 6   6♡      All Pass
♠ Q 9 8 6 3
♡ 5                                ^Forcing heart raise
◊ K 10 6 3                         Opening Lead: ♠ 6
♣ 9 4 2
```

At Trick 1, East played the ♠K, declarer won the ♠A.

Declarer cashed the ♣AK and ruffed a club high. He crossed to dummy with a trump and ruffed another club. He drew East's last trump and led the ♠10.

How should West continue?

West assumed declarer had eliminated clubs and spades. To avoid giving declarer a ruff/sluff, West switched to a diamond.

Was this a successful defense?

Did West count declarer's hand? With six hearts, two clubs, and two spades, how many diamonds? If only two, call the director, that's only twelve cards.

If declarer has three diamonds, one ruff/sluff won't help. If declarer has only two diamonds, the ◊AQ, he must have another spade. In either case, you can exit passively with another spade.

Don't get active and lead a diamond into declarer's doubleton ◊AQ.
Just wait to take the setting trick with your ◊K.

```
                              East
              South          ♠ K 7 4 2
              ♠ A 10         ♡ 4 3
              ♡ A Q 10 9 6 2 ◊ J 8 7
              ◊ A Q 5        ♣ Q J 8 3
              ♣ 7 5
```

Deal 68. Urgency

North	East	South	West	♠ A
1♣	P	1♠	P	♡ K Q 3
1NT	P	4♠	All Pass	◊ 10 9 6 3
				♣ Q J 10 4 2

Opening Lead: ◊ 2

East
♠ 7 5 2
♡ A J 8
◊ A J 7 4
♣ 8 7 6

East won the opening lead as declarer played the ◊Q.
How should East continue the defense?

East returned a diamond. Declarer ruffed Trick 2 and drew trumps. After losing a club finesse to West's king and knocking out the heart ace, declarer had ten tricks. Making four spades.

Where could the defense have found a fourth trick? Anywhere?

After winning Trick 1, East should see the threat of the second suit in the dummy and a need for urgency. Assuming partner has a trick, either a club or a trump but not both, the defense needs two heart tricks.

At Trick 2, East must return the ♡8, hoping West has the ♡10, which loses to one of dummy's honors. But if West wins a subsequent trick, a heart return means down one if declarer has three hearts.

West
♠ 9 6 3
♡ 10 7 5 2
◊ K 8 5 2
♣ K 5

South
♠ K Q J 10 8 4
♡ 9 6 4
◊ Q
♣ A 9 3

94

Deal 69. Entry Problems

North	East	South	West	♠ K
1♣	2♣	2◊	4♠	♡ K 6 2
P	P	5◊	All Pass	◊ J 5 3
				♣ A 10 9 8 5 4

Opening Lead: ♠ Jack

East
♠ A Q 6 5 3
♡ J 10 5 4
◊ void
♣ Q 6 3 2

Fierce competition pushed South into 5◊.

East won the ♠A. Seeing a second suit in dummy, how should East continue?

Seeing the second suit in dummy, East switched to the ♡J to attack the entry in dummy. Trick 2 went ♡J, 7, 3, K.

Declarer drew trumps and led a heart to his ♡9, making five diamonds. Ouch!

Active or passive? How should East defend?

If declarer can set up the clubs, there is no defense. But it's likely West has two clubs and declarer only one or West might have led one. Declarer may have two unavoidable heart losers.

IF East keeps his hands off the hearts, a passive spade return at Trick 2 means down one.

West
♠ J 10 8 7 4
♡ A 8 3
◊ 9 7 2
♣ K 7

South
♠ 9 2
♡ Q 9 7
◊ A K Q 10 8 6 4
♣ J

Deal 70. Good But Not Good

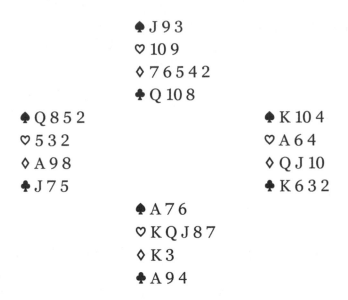

♠ J 9 3
♡ 10 9
◇ 7 6 5 4 2
♣ Q 10 8

♠ Q 8 5 2
♡ 5 3 2
◇ A 9 8
♣ J 7 5

♠ K 10 4
♡ A 6 4
◇ Q J 10
♣ K 6 3 2

♠ A 7 6
♡ K Q J 8 7
◇ K 3
♣ A 9 4

East opened 1♣ and South overcalled 1♡. West made a Negative Double showing exactly four spades. East bid 1NT. South, having misplaced his ◇3 in his hearts, rebid 2♡ which he thought was his six-card heart suit. Everyone passed.

West led the ♣ 5.

At Trick 1, declarer played low from dummy. How should East defend?

There is no reason for East to play the ♣K. South has the ♣A. West has not underled an ace. If East plays the ♣K, declarer will win the ♣A and later finesse West's ♣J. The ♣8 wins Trick 1 and in dummy, declarer leads the ◇2, 10, K, A.

How should West continue?

As passive as possible. Don't touch the clubs, just play back a diamond. East will win and play a third diamond which declarer ruffs. The diamonds are good, but declarer has no entry.

Declarer leads a trump, the ♡8. East wins and plays back....? A trump. Declarer is stuck. He wins the ♡10 in dummy but cannot use the good diamonds. The defenders still have trumps and declarer cannot attack clubs from the dummy.

South is held to seven tricks, down one.

Deal 71. Don't Be Fooled

North	East	South	West	♠ Q 10 8
1◊	1♡	1♠	P	♡ 9 3
2♠	Dbl	4♠	All Pass	◊ A K J 5 2
				♣ Q 4 3

♠ Q 10 8
♡ 9 3
◊ A K J 5 2
♣ Q 4 3

Opening Lead: ♡ 4 (count)

East
♠ 6 3
♡ A K Q 10 2
◊ Q 9 3
♣ A J 10

East won Trick 1 and continued a high heart.

Declarer played the ♡7, then the ♡J as West followed with the ♡6. How should East continue the defense?

At Trick 3, East could not return a club or diamond and he did not want to give declarer a ruff/sluff. East exited with a passive trump. Declarer played the ◊AK and ruffed a diamond.

He drew trumps ending in the dummy and cashed the remaining two diamonds, discarding a club and a heart. He conceded one club trick.

Making four spades.

East needed two club tricks. Should he have been fooled by declarer's discard?

Another high heart at Trick 3 would have removed the entry to the dummy.

If the ♡J was a true card, West started with ♡8654. At Trick 2, he would have played the 5 from 865, not the 6. The 6 was from 65 so declarer still had the 8.

There was no danger of a ruff/sluff. Good play by declarer.

West
♠ 7 5 2
♡ 6 5 4
◊ 8 7 6
♣ 8 7 6 2

South
♠ A K J 9 4
♡ J 8 7
◊ 10 4
♣ K 9 5

97

Deal 72. So Busy

South	West	North	East
1♠	P	1NT	P
4♠	All Pass		

♠ A 2
♡ J 10 8
◊ 8 7 5
♣ J 7 6 3 2

Opening Lead: ♣ 10

East
♠ 8 6 3
♡ 7 5 3
◊ A K J 4
♣ A Q 5

East won the opening lead with the ♣A as declarer played the ♣K.
How should East continue the defense?

East led the ◊K. When West play the deuce, East switched to the ♡7. Declarer won the ♡A, played the ♠K and a spade to the ♠A. Declarer led another diamond and East won the ◊A. Declarer won the heart return and drew the last trump. Making four spades.

Lucky lie of the cards or poor defense?

East was too busy. Dummy has only one entry. Should East be passive or active?
If declarer has diamond losers, he can't get rid of them. East should remain passive and return a heart at Trick 2.

In time, declarer will lose three diamond tricks if forced to play out of his hand.

West
♠ 5 4
♡ 9 6 4 2
◊ 10 3 2
♣ 10 9 8 4

South
♠ K Q J 10 9 7
♡ A K Q
◊ Q 9 6
♣ K

Deal 73. Following Orders

North	East	South	West
2♣	P	2◊^	P
2♠	P	2NT*	P
3♣	P	3♡#	P
3NT	All Pass		

♠ A K Q J 8
♡ 10
◊ K 5 2
♣ A K Q 6

^ Waiting * Negative
# Hoping North is 5=3=1=4
Opening Lead: ◊ J
Declarer played low from dummy and
Evelyn won the ◊A. Now what?

Evelyn
♠ 9 5 4
♡ K J 3
◊ A 9 7
♣ 10 7 4 2

I didn't have to look; I knew what was coming back. She returned the ◊9. Declarer claimed five spades, two diamonds, and four clubs.

"Evelyn, couldn't you see a diamond return gave him at least ten tricks?" I asked.
"That's the trouble with you, Jim," she said. "You tell me to return your suit and when I do you yell at me."

Evelyn's passive defense was a give-up. To have any chance to set the contract, the tricks have to come from the heart suit.

Declarer likely has five hearts or West would have led one. To unblock the suit, while retaining an entry to it, East's best return is the ♡J. Declarer will likely duck and East will continue with the ♡K, then the ♡3.
Four heart tricks, down one.

Jim - West
♠ 10 7 6 3
♡ A 9 7 2
◊ J 10 8
♣ 9 5

South
♠ 2
♡ Q 8 6 5 4
◊ Q 6 4 3
♣ J 8 3

Deal 74. I've Got You......

	♠ Q 10 9 2	South	West	North	East
	♡ Q 10 9 7	1♠	P	3♠^	P
	◇ A J 4	4♠		All Pass	
West	♣ 7 6		^ Limit Raise, four trump		
♠ A 3					
♡ 6 5 3 2			Opening Lead: ♣ Queen		
◇ Q 10 8					
♣ Q J 10 8					

Declarer played low from dummy, the ♣2 from East and declarer won the ♣A. At Trick 2, declarer led the ♠8 and West ducked.

The ♠Q in dummy won as East played the ♠4. Declarer played another spade. West won. Now what?

West played another club. Declarer won the ♣K and led the ♡A and a heart. In with the ♡K, East exited the ◇2 to West's queen and dummy's ace. Declarer discarded one diamond on dummy's long heart and conceded one diamond. Making four spades.

Could West have defended differently?

Marty Bergen showed this theme in the ACBL Bulletin, June 2017. West must appreciate that being passive is dangerous. A diamond switch at Trick 3 is necessary before the hearts are set up. But which diamond? Breaking new suits is delicate.

Leading the ◇8 or ◇Q will not do it if declarer has the ◇9. Bergen showed that only a "surrounding play", the ◇10 has a chance for two diamond tricks.

		East	♠ 6 4
			♡ K J
	South	♠ K J 8 7 5	◇ K 6 3 2
		♡ A 8 4	♣ 9 5 4 3 2
		◇ 9 7 5	
		♣ A K	

Marty said, "Surrounding plays are a lot of fun and kind of sexy. It's a technique that advancing players need to become familiar with." Thanks, Marty.

Deal 75. Assumptions

South	West	North	East	♠ K Q 6 4
1♠	P	2NT^	P	♡ 8 3
4♠	All Pass			◊ K Q 5

^ A Jacoby Forcing Spade Raise

Opening Lead: ♡ Jack

♠ K Q 6 4
♡ 8 3
◊ K Q 5
♣ Q J 10 9

East
♠ 9 5 2
♡ Q 6 2
◊ A J 9 7
♣ A 5 2

Declarer won the opening lead with the ♡A, East played the ♡6. After drawing trumps, declarer led a low club towards dummy. West played low and East won the ♣A. How should East continue?

East exited passively with the ♡Q. Declarer won the ♡ K and played another low club towards dummy. West won the ♣K and shifted to the ◊10. After East won the ◊A, declarer claimed. He discarded his remaining diamond loser on dummy's clubs.

Could East have defended differently?

To defeat the contract, East should assume she needs two clubs and two diamond tricks. But to get the diamonds before dummy's clubs are good, she needs to play West for not only the ♣K but also the......◊10.

After winning the ♣A, East must get active and return the ◊7. Dummy will win this trick with one diamond honor. When West wins the ♣K and leads the ◊6, East takes two diamond tricks. Declarer is down one.

West ♠ 8
♡ J 10 9 7 4
◊ 10 6 3
♣ K 8 6 3

South
♠ A J 10 7 3
♡ A K 5
◊ 8 4 2
♣ 7 4

Deal 76. Another Assumption

♠ K 8 4 2
♡ K 7
♦ A Q J 10
♣ K Q 9   EAST
            ♠ 6
            ♡ A J 10 9 6 4 3
            ♦ 9 4
            ♣ A J 5

East	South	West	North
1♡	2♠	3♡	4♠
All Pass			

Opening Lead: ♡ 2

Declarer plays the ♡K at Trick 1.

What should East lead after capturing dummy's ♡K with the ♡A?

East counted two aces in his hand. Perhaps West had a trump trick. East tried another heart. Declarer ruffed and led a spade. West won the ♠A and led a club to dummy's ♣K and East's ♣A. Declarer claimed. Making four spades.

Was there a fourth trick for the defense?

Yes, with a more active line of defense. Returning a passive heart at Trick 2 was futile. The opening lead marked West with three hearts. East, starring at dummy's good diamonds, should know the only hope was two club tricks.

If West had a fast entry in trumps, there was a chance. East should return the ♣5 at Trick 2. West's ♣10 forces out one of dummy's club honors. When West wins the ♠A, his ♣2 return gives East two club tricks. Down one.

West
♠ A 7
♡ Q 5 2
♦ 8 7 5 3
♣ 10 7 6 2   South
                ♠ Q J 10 9 5 3
                ♡ 8
                ♦ K 6 2
                ♣ 8 4 3

Deal 77. Durocher to Lazzeri to Gehrig

Joe Dugan
♠ A Q
♡ K Q J 10
◊ 8 5 3
♣ K Q J 7

North	South
1♡	1♠
2NT	3♣
4♠	All Pass

Leo Durocher
♠ 6
♡ 9 7 6 5
◊ A K Q 6 4
♣ 5 4 2

Tony Lazzeri
♠ 8 5 3 2
♡ A 4 3 2
◊ 9 2
♣ 10 9 8

Lou Gehrig
♠ K J 10 9 7 4
♡ 8
◊ J 10 7
♣ A 6 3

Contract Bridge was less than three years old when this deal arose.

Leo led the ◊K and cashed the ◊Q at Trick 2. When he led the ◊A to Trick 3, Tony wondered whether to request a heart shift with the ♡4, the highest he could spare, or discourage clubs with the ♣8, his lowest.

Having clubbed a then-record 60 home runs in a Texas League season before joining the Yankees, Tony naturally chose the ♣8. Whereupon Leo shifted to the ♣5. Curtains! Lou won the ♣A, drew trumps and claimed ten tricks (six spades and four clubs) to make 4♠.

As soon as Lou claimed, Leo gave Tony some lip: "Why didn't you ruff my ace of diamonds and cash the ace of hearts?"

Tony remembered the last time he'd trumped Leo's ace. The tongue lashing he'd received wasn't pleasant. "I figured you're so smart, Leo, you'd know what to do, so I just threw my lowest card in a suit I didn't want led."

Eventually, they agreed to let Gehrig be the judge. Can you guess what Lou said?

"If you're so smart, Leo, why didn't you lead a low diamond to Trick 3 to force Tony to ruff. Couldn't you rely on Tony to know which ace he had?"
By Danny Kleinman

Deal 78. Hard to Find

South	West	North	East	♠ Q J 10 7
1♣	1♠	Dbl^	2♠	♡ K 10 8 6
3♡	All Pass			◊ 9 2
^ Negative, 4+ hearts				♣ 8 5 3
Opening Lead: ♣ 6				East
				♠ A 3 2
				♡ 9 3
				◊ J 10 8 6 5
				♣ Q 6 4

Declarer made a good play at Trick 1, playing low from dummy. If the lead was fourth best, East had the ♣A, West the ♣K. East won the ♣A. How should East continue?

With his own suit now a threat, returning a spade was out. Was this a crossruff deal? Perhaps a trump? He returned the ♡3, both passive and active.

Declarer drew trumps ending in dummy and led the ♠Q. Instead of ruffing, he discarded a club, a loser-on-loser play.

Declarer had nine tricks: He had four hearts in hand, two spades in dummy, the club ace, the diamond queen, and one ruff in dummy.

Could East have defended differently?

East could not prevent declarer from setting up the spades, but he needs to shift to a minor at Trick 2. He needs less from partner in clubs than in diamonds.

A club shift at Trick 2 defeats three hearts. On a crossruff, declarer has too many losers. But a good use by declarer of the Rule of Eleven at Trick 1.

West	♠ K 9 8 6 5		
	♡ J 5 4		
	◊ A 4		
	♣ K 10 9	South	
		♠ 4	
		♡ A Q 7 2	
		◊ K Q 7 3	
		♣ A J 7 2	

104

Deal 79. Creating Danger

South	West	North	East
1♡	1♠	3♡	3♠
4♡	All Pass		

♠ 7 4
♡ Q 8 7 4 3
◊ 6 5
♣ Q J 6 5

Opening Lead: ♠ Q

East
♠ K 10 8
♡ 6
◊ Q J 9 4 3 2
♣ 8 3 2

At Trick 1, declarer played low from dummy.
How should East defend?

East played an encouraging ♠8 and declarer played low. West continued a spade and declarer won Trick 2 with the ♠A. After drawing trumps in two rounds, declarer lost a club finesse to West's ♣K.

But West was the safe hand and could not attack diamonds. Declarer had time to cash the clubs and discard one diamond loser. A danger hand, well played at Trick 1 by declarer.

Can we say the same for East?

No. East was too passive. If East overtakes West's ♠Q with his ♠K at Trick 1, declarer has no winning options. If he ducks, East will switch to the ◊Q. If declarer wins Trick 1, West can cross to East's ♠10 later for the diamond play.

West
♠ Q J 9 6 3
♡ 10 2
◊ A 10 7
♣ K 7 4

South
♠ A 5 2
♡ A K J 9 5
◊ K 8
♣ A 10 9

Deal 80. No Air, Please

```
              ♠ J 9 2        South  West  North    East
              ♡ A 8 6        1NT    P     3NT      All Pass
              ◇ K Q 6 5
West          ♣ Q 7 3        Opening Lead: ♡ 3
♠ 7
♡ J 7 5 3 2
◇ A 10 9 8
♣ A 9 2
```

Declarer captured East's ♡9 at Trick 1 with the ♡K and led the ◇2. West played low and dummy's king won. Declarer crossed to his hand with the ♠A and led another low diamond.

How should West continue the defense?

Aces are for capturing kings, or at least honor cards. Play low again. Dummy's queen wins as East shows out. Declarer was hoping for 3-2 diamonds or the ace capturing air. Declarer plays a diamond to his jack.

Now what?

Win and cash two diamond tricks and exit with? A low club? The club ace?

No, no, no. Just stay passive with another heart. Whoever plays clubs first loses out. When declarer, with only eight tricks, leads a club, as long as neither defender captures air with his honor, declarer cannot find a ninth trick.

```
                                East
                                ♠ 10 8 6 5 4 3
                                ♡ 10 9
                                ◇ 3
               South            ♣ K 10 6 5
               ♠ A K Q
               ♡ K Q 4
               ◇ J 7 4 2
               ♣ J 8 4
```

Deal 81. Can You Count?

	♠ 5 3	South	West	North	East
	♡ A K Q 10	1◊	P	1♡	1♠
	◊ J 10 7	1NT	P	3NT	All Pass
West	♣ Q 7 4 2				
♠ 10 6 2		Opening Lead: ♠ 2			
♡ 6 5					
◊ Q 6 5 3 2					
♣ K J 8					

At Trick 1, East played the ♠K and declarer won the ace.

Declarer continued with the ◊A and East showed out, discarding a low heart. Declarer next led a low diamond.

How should West continue the defense?

West won and continued a passive defense, leading the ♠10. Do you think this was successful? The passive spade return let South take four diamonds, two spades, and four hearts.

Who has the ♣Q? Who has the ♣A? Why?

If East had the ♣Q, he would not have played the ♠K at Trick 1.

What are South's HCP? ♠AQ and ◊AK so far, and most likely from East's discard the ♡J.

The ♣A would give South 17-18 HCP, far too strong for his bidding. So East has it. Shift to clubs, starting with the ♣J to avoid blocking the suit, and continue with the ♣K if the ♣J holds.

This active defense gives the defenders four club tricks and one diamond trick. Passive here is giving up. You can count, can't you?

	East
	♠ K J 9 8 4
South	♡ 9 8 4 3
♠ A Q 7	◊ void
♡ J 7 2	♣ A 10 9 5
◊ A K 9 8 4	
♣ 6 3	

107

Deal 82. Don't Defrost It

	♠ J 8 6 3	South	West	North	East
	♡ K J 10	1♠	P	2♠	P
	◊ Q 10 5 4	4♠		All Pass	
West	♣ A 6				
♠ 10 5 2					
♡ 9 5		Opening Lead: Choose it
◊ J 7 6 2					
♣ 9 8 4 2					

You could make a case for a trump, top of a doubleton, a fourth best diamond or a worthless club? West chose the ♡9.

Good (lucky?) choice. East wins the ♡AQ at Tricks 1 and 2 and returns the ♡8 for West to ruff. How should West continue? A diamond? The ♡8 was a high heart, suggesting a diamond return.

The contract is tight meaning you only need one more trick. There is rarely a rush to grab it. You can usually just get off lead and wait.

What you must not do is open up suits that may be frozen. Suits where whoever goes first loses a trick. Two typical examples:

	K95			J43	
Q84		A106	K97		A1052
	J732			Q86	

East-West will take only one trick if they go first. North-South will damage themselves if they go first.

In the above deal, if East has the ◊A it's not going away. West must exit passively - a club. Eventually the defense will score a diamond trick. Down one.

	East ♠ 9
	♡ A Q 8 4 3
South	◊ K 8 3
♠ A K Q 7 4	♣ J 7 5 3
♡ 7 6 2	
◊ A 9	
♣ K Q 10	

Deal 83. Just Go Low

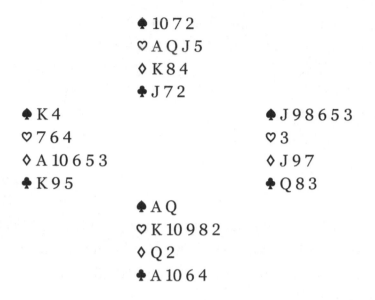

♠ 10 7 2
♡ A Q J 5
◊ K 8 4
♣ J 7 2

♠ K 4
♡ 7 6 4
◊ A 10 6 5 3
♣ K 9 5

♠ J 9 8 6 5 3
♡ 3
◊ J 9 7
♣ Q 8 3

♠ A Q
♡ K 10 9 8 2
◊ Q 2
♣ A 10 6 4

South reached 4♡ after a 1♡ - 3♡ - 4♡ auction.

First question: What should West lead? He knows North has ten to eleven HCP and South has extra values. With his ten quality HCP, East must have few values.
West leads the ♡4.

A passive lead is best. Might this pickle partner's trump holding? Nah, unless it's a singleton behind declarer's ♡A and declarer guesses to pick it off.

Declarer drew trumps and led a low diamond towards the king. West played low, passive, and the king won. Declarer tried the spade finesse. West won and returned a spade, passive, not wanting to break another suit.

Declarer exited the ◊Q to West. West returned a diamond, passive, which declarer ruffed. Notice how neither side wanted to start the club suit.

But now declarer had little choice. He had to start the clubs and had to lose two tricks. As long as the defense was on its toes, low from West if declarer led low from hand, or East covered the jack if led from dummy, declarer was down one.

Deal 84. Full Speed Ahead

South	West	North	East	♠ 6 4 2
1♡	P	2♡	P	♡ K 9 5 2
4♡	All Pass			◊ Q J 6
				♣ Q 9 5 Jim

Opening Leas: ♠ King

      ♠ 9 8 7
      ♡ 8 4
      ◊ 9 8 4
      ♣ A 10 8 4 2

As soon as the dummy came down and I saw the opening lead, I was ready to fold my cards and concede. I had the only card in my hand that was going to give declarer the contract. After all, I was playing with Evelyn. I had no chance.

Do you know which card?

If the hand was cold, nothing mattered. But if declarer had two spade losers, he was going to duck Trick 1 and hope West continued spades. And Evelyn was going to see which card I played at Trick 1. Yes, you got it! And with her a seven or higher is encouraging, a six or lower is discouraging. Period, end of story.

With Evelyn, it's full speed ahead; damn the torpedoes.

Of course, the 2, 3, 4, 5, and 6 were all exposed or would be at Trick 1. No matter, a seven is high. Evelyn continued with the ♠Q, making four hearts.

There is no sense in playing that a seven or higher is encouraging. You can only signal with the cards you have been dealt. There was no point in even discussing this with Evelyn. On to the next deal.

Like I said, I could have folded up at Trick 1. I saw it coming.

Evelyn – West   ♠ K Q 10 5
              ♡ 10 6
              ◊ 10 7 3 2
              ♣ K J 7   South

                       ♠ A J 3
                       ♡ A Q J 7 3
                       ◊ A K 5
                       ♣ 6 3

Deal 85. Third Try is a Charm

South	West	North	East
1♥	P	2♦	P
2♥	P	4♥	All Pass

♠ 5 4
♥ A Q 5
♦ A Q J 10 5
♣ 9 7 5

Opening Lead: ♠ Queen

East
♠ A 9 7 6 2
♥ 7 4 2
♦ 9 6
♣ Q 6 4

East won the opening lead.

How should he continue the defense?

East returned a passive spade. Declarer, the Devil, won the ♠K and drew trumps. He discarded his club losers on the long diamonds.

"Want to try again?" asked the Devil. "But if you get it wrong again, your soul is mine."

East went active and switched to the ♣4. The Devil played low from his hand and West won the ♣10. The best West could do was cash the ♣A to hold the Devil to ten tricks.

"You are mine," said the Devil. "One more try," begged East.

"They don't call me 'Lucifer M. Mephistopheles' for nothing," said the Devil. "The 'M' stands for 'Merciful'."

West
♠ Q J 10 8
♥ 6
♦ 8 4 3 2
♣ A J 10 2

The Devil
♠ K 3
♥ K J 10 9 8 3
♦ K 7
♣ K 8 3

To beat the Devil, East must switch to the club queen at Trick 2. The defense needs three quick club tricks and East must play West for the ♣AJ10 to prevent the Devil from ducking Trick 2.

"Foiled again," said the Devil.

Deal 86. Don't Touch

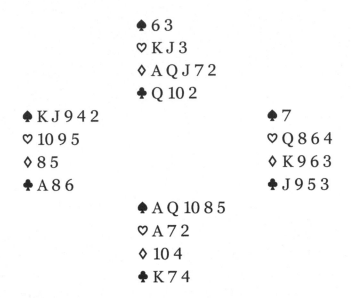

♠ 6 3
♥ K J 3
♦ A Q J 7 2
♣ Q 10 2

♠ K J 9 4 2
♥ 10 9 5
♦ 8 5
♣ A 8 6

♠ 7
♥ Q 8 6 4
♦ K 9 6 3
♣ J 9 5 3

♠ A Q 10 8 5
♥ A 7 2
♦ 10 4
♣ K 7 4

South opened 1♠ and North forced to game, bidding 2♦. South rebid 2NT and North bid 3NT.

What should West lead? Had the auction gone 1NT – 3NT, West would surely lead fourth from his longest and strongest, the ♠4. Why not? But knowing declarer has five spades makes a spade lead verboten. Hearts or clubs?

It's always better to not lead from an ace. That almost always blows a trick and partner's return destroys an entry. West led the ♥ 10.

Declarer played low and won the ♥A in hand. He led the ♦10; everyone played low (good duck by East). East won the second diamond and returned a spade, knowing partner was sitting behind declarer with five spades.

West won the ♠K and continued with a passive ♥9. Declarer finessed the ♥J, losing to East's queen. East returned a passive heart.

By staying passive, declarer was held to eight tricks.

Down one.

Deal 87. Worth a Try

South	West	North	East
2NT	P	4♡^	P
4♠	All Pass		

^ Texas transfer to spades

Opening Lead: ◊ Queen

♠ Q 10 7 5 4 3
♡ J 10 2
◊ 9 7 3
♣ 2

East
♠ J 9 2
♡ A 5
◊ A 10 6 5 2
♣ J 10 4.

A deal from the World Team Championships in Beijing some years ago. At many tables, East won the ◊ A.

How should East continue?

East returned a diamond. Declarer won and drew trumps. Making four spades.

Passive or active? We saw what passive brought.

At some tables, East realized a diamond continuation was futile. South was marked with the ◊K. There was room in the West hand for only a few HCP.

East wondered, "Which few high-card points could beat the contract?" Picturing West with three, four, or five hearts to the king, East played the ♡A and received an encouraging ♡9 from West.

East continued a heart to West's ♡K and ruffed the heart continuation.

Down one.

West
♠ 6
♡ K 9 8 6
◊ Q J 8
♣ 9 8 7 6 5

South
♠ A K 8
♡ Q 7 4 3
◊ K 4
♣ A K Q 3

Deal 88. No Double, No Trouble

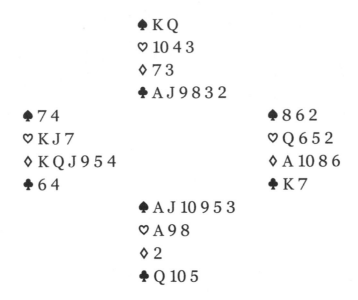

```
                    ♠ K Q
                    ♡ 10 4 3
                    ◇ 7 3
                    ♣ A J 9 8 3 2
♠ 7 4                                   ♠ 8 6 2
♡ K J 7                                 ♡ Q 6 5 2
◇ K Q J 9 5 4                           ◇ A 10 8 6
♣ 6 4                                   ♣ K 7
                    ♠ A J 10 9 5 3
                    ♡ A 9 8
                    ◇ 2
                    ♣ Q 10 5
```

South opened 1♠ and West overcalled 2◇. North's 3♣ overbid was game forcing. East took advantage of the favorable vulnerability and bid 5◇. "No one steals from me," thought South, bidding 5♠. He was lucky, everyone quietly passed. West led the ◇ K.

East played the ◇10. What did that mean? More diamonds? A suit preference for hearts? Unsure, West continued another passive diamond. Declarer ruffed, drew trumps, and lost a club finesse to East.

East switched to a low heart, but it was too late. Declarer won the ♡A and threw his heart losers on the good clubs in dummy. Making five spades.

Asses the blame between East and West?

West might have considered a heart shift at Trick 2 starring at those clubs in dummy. But East's values might have included ♣KQx instead of the ♡Q.

It was strictly up to East to find a heart shift. Instead of sitting passively by, overtake the ◇K with the ◇A at Trick 1 and make the heart switch himself. When he wins the club king, the defense can cash two heart tricks for down two.

Of course, East yelled first "Why didn't you switch at Trick 2?"
He who yells first is usually the one who is wrong

114

Deal 89. Play It Safe

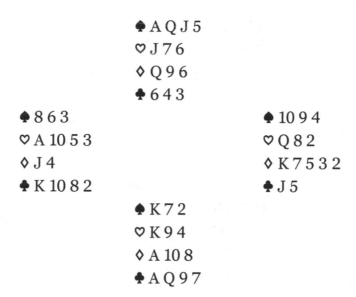

♠ A Q J 5
♡ J 7 6
◇ Q 9 6
♣ 6 4 3

♠ 8 6 3
♡ A 10 5 3
◇ J 4
♣ K 10 8 2

♠ 10 9 4
♡ Q 8 2
◇ K 7 5 3 2
♣ J 5

♠ K 7 2
♡ K 9 4
◇ A 10 8
♣ A Q 9 7

Playing safe is often your best strategy. After you see dummy or declarer's line of play, often your goal will be to avoid leading anything that might give away a trick.

When the opening leader does not have a five-card suit, safety is often best. This allows a defender to visualize the dummy before committing to an active defense. What should West lead in the above deal after a 1NT – 3NT auction?

The auction suggests they have the minors. I like the ♠8.

Yes, sometimes these seemingly safe leads from three small are an illusion and often pickle partner's holding in the suit.

Imagine East with ♠ Qxx ♡ 98x ◇ Qxxx ♣ Qxx. Here a spade lead may be costly and a ♣2 effective. Good days, bad days.

Dummy's ♠J wins Trick 1. Declarer leads the ♣3 to his ♣9 and your ♣10.
Now what? Time to go active? Switch to a heart or diamond?

No, no, and no. Declarer must be struggling if he had to take a deep club finesse. East must have something in clubs. Let him keep struggling. Just stay passive and return another spade. Render unto Caesar, etc.

Wait for declarer to come to you. If you break a new suit, you give declarer his ninth trick. Ouch.

Deal 90. Overcoming Futility

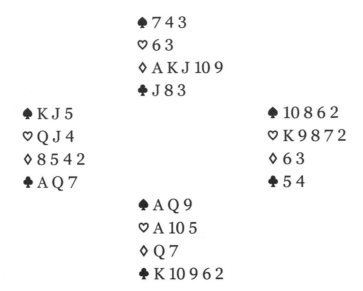

♠ 7 4 3
♡ 6 3
◊ A K J 10 9
♣ J 8 3

♠ K J 5
♡ Q J 4
◊ 8 5 4 2
♣ A Q 7

♠ 10 8 6 2
♡ K 9 8 7 2
◊ 6 3
♣ 5 4

♠ A Q 9
♡ A 10 5
◊ Q 7
♣ K 10 9 6 2

After a 1NT-3NT auction, West led the ♡Q and continued the ♡J as both held, East signaling high-low and declarer following with the ♡5 and ♡10. Since West could count thirteen HCP in his hand, he knew East had only the ♡K.

Another heart would set up the heart suit, but East was never getting in.

West hoping for some miracle, continued a futile heart.

Declarer won, went to dummy with a diamond and passed the ♣8 to the ♣Q. West returned a diamond. South knocked out the ♣A, being lucky to find that card with West, and made 3NT.

Would you have given up or was there a possible successful defense?

Frank Stewart showed a spectacular defense in his terrific newspaper column a few years ago. West recognized the futility of a passive third round of hearts. West could count nine tricks for declarer if he had four or more clubs as he could set up two club tricks.

So the race was on. Hoping for a layout in which East held ♠10xx or longer, West shifted to the ♠K.

"Thanks," said South, smiling. Declarer started the clubs. West won the ♣Q and led the ♠J. South wasn't smiling anymore, he still had only eight tricks.

When West won the ♣A, a spade to East's ♠10 was the setting trick.

Two hearts, two clubs, and one spade. Thanks, Frank.

Deal 91. Proper Switch

East	South	West	North	♠ K 9 6	
1NT	3♠	P	4♠	♡ 9 5 3	
All Pass				◊ A 9 7 5 2	
				♣ K J	East

Opening Lead: ♣ 2   ♠ 7 2

East won the first two club tricks.   ♡ K J

How should East continue the defense?   ◊ K Q 10 3

                                                       ♣ A Q 9 6 4

East switched to the ♡K, thinking this was an aggressive play against the threatening diamond suit. Declarer won the ♡A, played the ◊4 to the ◊A and ruffed a diamond with a middle trump. Declarer then led the ♠8: Q, K. He ruffed another small diamond with a middle trump and led a trump to dummy's nine.

After one more diamond ruff, the spade six was the entry to the good fifth diamond to discard a heart. He lost two clubs and one heart.

What was the better defense?

Just the opposite. As usual, hand pattern recognition. What kind of hand did this rate to be? Yes, a second suit. And what's the best defense to a second suit hand?

Attack the entries. And East should see that could only mean trumps.

A trump return at Trick 3 upsets the timing before declarer is ready to start setting up the diamonds.

```
West
♠ Q
♡ Q 10 7 6 2
◊ J 8 6
♣ 10 8 3 2        South
                  ♠ A J 10 8 5 4 3
                  ♡ A 8 4
                  ◊ 4
                  ♣ 7 5
```

While a trump return at Trick 3 looked passive, it was actually the correct aggressive play.

Deal 92. An Elusive Fourth Trick

South	West	North	East	♠ Q J 9
1♡	P	2◊	P	♡ Q 10 6
3◊	P	3♡	P	◊ K 10 9 6 3
4♡	All Pass			♣ K Q

♠ 7 6 5 3
♡ 4 3
◊ A 7 5
♣ A 8 6 5

Opening Lead: ♣ J

East won Trick 1. How should he continue?

Not wanting to break any suits, he returned a passive small club. Declarer drew trumps, knocking out two aces and made his contract - four hearts.

Routine? Was there a better line of defense?

Yes, if East gave the hand more thought. Sometimes doing nothing is good but there are times you have to get active. At Trick 2, East should have been trying to figure out where four tricks were coming from.

West probably has one good card. If a high heart, that's three tricks. Maybe a high spade? If West had a singleton diamond, he would have led it. But possibly a doubleton diamond? Very likely on the bidding.

At Trick 2, East led a low diamond. Yes! When West won the first trump, he returned his remaining diamond to East's ◊A. The subsequent diamond ruff was the setting trick. Well done!

West
♠ 10 4 2
♡ A 5 2
◊ 4 2
♣ J 10 9 4 3

Perhaps with trump control, West might have led the top of his worthless doubleton. Usually not a good lead without trump control.

South
♠ A K 8
♡ K J 9 8 7
◊ Q J 8
♣ 7 2

Deal 93. Timing

North	East	South	West
1♠	P	2♡	P
3♡	P	4♡	All Pass

♠ K J 10 6 5
♡ K 9 5
◊ 7 3
♣ A J 3

Opening Lead: ◊ Q

East won the opening lead.
How should East continue?

East
♠ 9 3 2
♡ 8 2
◊ A 9 8 5 2
♣ K 10 2

East returned the ◊2 to declarer's ◊K. East then sat back to wait for his ♣K. He was going to have a long wait. Declarer drew the trumps and forced out West's ♠A. He discarded his two losing clubs on dummy's good spades.

What could the defense have done differently?

Active or passive? A good defender has the ability to distinguish when he can sit back and wait from the times he needs to get busy. On this deal, the sight of the second suit in dummy suggests quick action. West can have one quick trick but where is the setting trick?

It can only come from the club suit. East must hope West has the ♣Q and return the ♣2 at Trick 2 before the spades are established.

West
♠ A 8 4
♡ 7 3
◊ Q J 10 4
♣ Q 8 6 4

South
♠ Q 7
♡ A Q J 10 6 4
◊ K 6
♣ 9 7 5

The defense takes one spade, one diamond, and two clubs. Down one.

Deal 94. False Attitude

		South	West	North	East
♠ J		South	West	North	East
♡ 6 4 2		1♠	P	2♣	P
◊ J 10 6		2♡	P	3♣	P
♣ A K Q J 7 4		3♠	P	4♠	All Pass

♠ Q 9 6 5
♡ Q 10 7 5   Opening Lead: ◊ A, playing A from AKx opening leads
◊ A K 9   East followed to Trick 1 with an encouraging ◊8.
♣ 10 2   How should West continue the defense?

West, seeing two or three more tricks in his hand, continued with a passive ◊K, ruffed by declarer. Declarer led a low spade to the ♠J which held, then the ♡2 to his ♡A. He played the ♠AK and another spade. West won the ♠Q but the declarer had the rest. He lost one diamond and one spade.

Could the defenders have found a way to defeat four spades?

Yes, if both defenders had appreciated the danger of dummy's running clubs and the need to kill the entry to them – the club suit itself. East can tell a diamond continuation will be ruffed. If West had ◊AK doubleton, he would have led the king. So East should discourage with the ◊2 at Trick 1.

Then West would see his one spade and two heart tricks as the setting tricks. Instead of a passive diamond, he will attack clubs at Trick 2 and rise with the ♠Q to lead another club. Then he can sit back and wait for his two heart tricks to beat four spades. Declarer has no entry to dummy.

East
♠ 3 2
♡ 8 3
◊ Q 8 5 4 3 2
♣ 9 8 6

South
♠ A K 10 8 7 4
♡ A K J 9
◊ 7
♣ 5 3

Deal 95. Which Door?

		North	East	South	West
♠ A 6 4		North	East	South	West
♡ K 10 3 2		1♣	P	1♡	P
◊ A J 5		2♡	All Pass		
♣ Q 7 2					

West
♠ K Q J 2
♡ Q 8 4
◊ 8 7 3
♣ K 9 4

Opening Lead: ♠ K

Declarer wins Trick 1 with the ♠A. He cashes the ♡K and plays a heart back to his ♡J and West's ♡Q. West cashes the ♠QJ as everyone follows.

How should West continue? A club or a diamond? Door 1 or Door 2?

If you exited thru Door 1, clubs or Door 2, diamonds, declarer made two hearts. Left on his own, declarer had to lose two club tricks and guess the diamond queen.

Whichever minor West exited in solved one of declarer's problems.

How should West have defended at Trick 6?

Find Door 3. Exit passively with his last trump and let declarer do his own work.

He may or may not make two hearts. But why are you helping him? Who are you – the Red Cross coming to his rescue?

East
♠ 10 8 3
♡ 7 5
◊ Q 9 6 4
♣ A 10 8 3

South
♠ 9 7 5
♡ A J 9 6
◊ K 10 2
♣ J 6 5

Deal 96. Annoying

East	South	West	North	♠ A J 8 7
1♦	3♠	P	6♠	♡ A 5
All Pass				♦ 6 5 2
				♣ A Q 10 9

♠ A J 8 7
♡ A 5
♦ 6 5 2
♣ A Q 10 9

Opening Lead: ♦ 9

East
♠ 5 4
♡ K J 7
♦ A K Q J 10
♣ K J 7

You, East have a really good hand. You opened the bidding with high hopes and the opponents bid a slam like you weren't even there.

And then declarer ruffed the opening lead. Annoying! Declarer led the ♠3 to dummy, West showed out, and ruffed another diamond. Then the ♠6 to dummy was followed by ruffing the last diamond.

Declarer next led the ♣2 to dummy's ♣Q and your king. Now what?

Dummy has left ♠ 8 7 ♡ A 5 ♦ none ♣ A 10 9

You have left ♠ none ♡ K J 7 ♦ A K ♣ J 7

East exited the ♡7. Was this successful?

How could East have known the proper defense?

East needed to stay passive and return a club into the ♣A109. Count declarer's tricks. Seven spades, three clubs in dummy, and the heart ace for eleven.

If East doesn't panic, declarer will lose a trick to East's ♡K.

West
♠ void
♡ 10 8 3 2
♦ 9 8 7 4 3
♣ 6 5 4 3

South
♠ K Q 10 9 6 3 2
♡ Q 9 6 4
♦ void
♣ 8 2

Deal 97. Play For What You Need

North	East	South	West
1♣	P	1♡	P
3♠^	P	4♡	All Pass

♠ K
♡ A J 5 2
♢ A Q 6
♣ K J 10 9 6

^ Splinter, hearts with spade shortness

Opening Lead: ♠ Q

East
♠ A 8 5 2
♡ 8 4
♢ K 8 5 2
♣ A Q 7

At Trick 1, East captured dummy's king with his ♠A.

How should East continue the defense?

East returned a trump at Trick 2. Declarer won, drew trumps, and led a club to dummy's ♣J. East won the ♣Q and returned a spade. Declarer ruffed in dummy and forced out the ♣A. He ruffed the next spade and claimed, throwing his diamond losers on the good clubs.

Could the defense have found a fourth trick?

East was annoyed partner had not found a diamond lead but as we have said, the defense can often overcome one slip, but not two. Needing a diamond trick, and needing one quickly, East must assume West has the ♢J9x.

If East returns a diamond at Trick 2, into the teeth of dummy's ♢AQ6, the defenders can build a diamond trick before dummy's clubs are good.

Declarer is down one. Play for what you need to defeat a contract.

West
♠ Q J 9 6 3
♡ 6 3
♢ J 9 4
♣ 8 3 2

South
♠ 10 7 4
♡ K Q 10 9 7
♢ 10 7 3
♣ 5 4

Deal 98. Percentage Play

South	West	North	East
1♡	P	1♠	P
2♡	P	3♡	P
4♡	All Pass		

♠ A 7 6 5 2
♡ 10 2
◊ K 5 3
♣ A 7 3

Opening Lead: ◊ J

♠ K 10 9 3
♡ 8 5
◊ A Q 7 6
♣ 10 9 6

The ◊J held the first trick. West continued with the ◊10, winning, and a third diamond.

How should East defend?

When West continued a third diamond, declarer ruffed and drew trumps. Declarer's plan was to set up the spades in dummy rather than taking a 50% finesse. If spades were no worse than 4-2, an 84% chance, he would not need the club finesse.

At Trick 4, he played a low spade from both hands, preserving an entry. Then using the trump ten and the two black aces in dummy, it was easy to set up the fifth spade to discard the club loser.

How should East-West have defended against four hearts?

Better defense by East is to overtake the diamond at Trick 2, and switch to the club ten, attacking the entry in dummy before declarer can start the spades.

West
♠ Q J
♡ 7 6 4
◊ J 10 9 8
♣ Q 8 5 2

South
♠ 8 4
♡ A K Q J 9 3
◊ 4 2
♣ K J 4

Deal 99. Back At'ya

Sometimes there is a suit combination you don't want to touch. As we have seen, it's best to make the defenders go first. But sometimes they can throw the ball back to you. Mike Lawrence showed this theme some time ago on his excellent BridgeClues website.

K J 4

? 9 8 6   ? 3 2

10 7 5

Declarer could only afford to lose one trick in this combination. His best play was to endplay East into breaking the suit. A defensive slip would see him home.

♠ Q J 9 4
♡ K J 4
◊ 10 8
♣ A 7 3 2

♠ 6 3   ♠ 5
♡ Q 9 8 6   ♡ A 3 2
◊ K 9 4 3   ◊ A 7 6 5 2
♣ Q J 10   ♣ 9 6 5 4

♠ A K 10 8 7 2
♡ 10 7 5
◊ Q J
♣ K 8

South reached 4♠ after a 1 – 3 – 4 auction. West led the ♣ Q.

Declarer won the ♣K, cashed the ♠A, and led to the ♣A. He ruffed a club and led to the ♠Q. After ruffing the last club, he exited in diamonds.

West won the ◊K and led to East's ◊A. East led the ♡2. Declarer played low. How should West defend from here? ♡Q or ♡9?

West needs partner to have the ♡A or it's all over. Declarer shape is known to be 6=3=2=2. If West plays the ♡Q, declarer loses one trick, the ace.

West must play the ♡9, putting the ball back in declarer's hands to play the rest of the suit himself. Declarer must lose two tricks. Down one. Thanks, Mike.

Deal 100. A Logical Inference

South	West	North	East
1NT	P	2♡^	P
2♠	P	3NT	P
4♠	All Pass		

^ Transfer to Spades

Opening Lead: ◊ J

♠ K J 10 7 2
♡ K 10 2
◊ K 6 5
♣ 6 3

East
♠ Q 5 4
♡ A 5
◊ 8 4 2
♣ Q 10 7 4 2

Declarer won the opening lead in hand with the ◊A and led the ♠9, playing low from dummy. East won the ♠Q. How should East continue the defense?

East returned a passive small diamond. Declarer won and continued trumps, forcing out the ♠A. After knocking out the ♡A, he claimed. Declarer lost two trump tricks and the heart ace. Making four spades.

Did the defense miss anything? What inference did East fail to appreciate?

If declarer had ♠A9x, why did he not cash the ♠A at Trick 2 before taking a finesse for the ♠Q? An alert East will cash the ♡A and play his last heart at Tricks 3 and 4.

When West wins the next trump lead with the ♠A, West can give East a heart ruff, the setting trick.

West
♠ A 3
♡ 8 7 6 4
◊ J 10 9 7
♣ J 9 5

South
♠ 9 8 6
♡ Q J 9 3
◊ A Q 3
♣ A K 8

Deal 101. Urgent

East	South	West	North	
1♦	2♣	P	2♠	♠ A Q 6 5 2
P	3♣	P	3♦	♡ 8 7
P	5♣	All Pass		♦ Q 10 7
				♣ 8 5 4

Opening Lead: ♦ 2

East won Trick 1 with the ♦J.
How should East continue?

East
♠ J 9
♡ K 10 9 5
♦ A K J 4 3
♣ 3 2

East cashed the ♦K, then tried to cash the ♦A. South ruffed the diamond high and cashed the ♣AK, West following once.

Declarer then played the spade king, a spade to the ace and ruffed a spade high. Using the preserved ♣6, he crossed to dummy's ♣8 and discarded his two losing hearts on the good spades.

Making five clubs, off the first four tricks! Whose fault was this tragedy?

100% East. He knew the third diamond was not cashing from West's carding. Seeing dummy's spades, a passive defense won't do. A heart switch was urgent.

West
♠ 10 7 4 3
♡ A Q J 3 2
♦ 9 6 2
♣ 7

South
♠ K 8
♡ 6 4
♦ 8 5
♣ A K Q J 10 9 6

Deal 102. Don't Tell

South	West	North	East	♠ Q 9
1◊	P	1♡	P	♡ A Q 8 4 3 2
3♣	P	3♡	P	◊ 8 7 2
4♣	P	4◊	P	♣ 9 5
5◊	All Pass			

East

♠ A K 7 5
♡ K 9 6
◊ J 6 4 3
♣ J 3

Opening Lead: ♠ 3

East won the ♠AK. How should he continue the defense?

East switched to a passive club jack. Declarer won and cashed the ◊AK. When West showed out on the second round of trumps, declarer led the ♡5 to dummy's ♡A and finessed East's ◊J with his ◊Q9.

Making five diamonds.

How could the defense have defeated five diamonds?

East, after winning Tricks 1 and 2, should think about the bidding. Since South rated to have a singleton heart, switch to the ♡6 into dummy's ♡AQ8432 before declarer discovers the bad trump split.

No trump finesse for this declarer. Down one. Maybe South should have been suspicious after that heart play at Trick 3 and take a first round finesse? Tough.

West ♠ 10 8 6 3 2
♡ J 10 7
◊ 5
♣ 8 7 4 2

South
♠ J 4
♡ 5
◊ A K Q 10 9
♣ A K Q 10 6

Deal 103. Leave Him Alone

South	West	North	East	♠ Q 10 6 2
1♠	P	3♠^	P	♡ A 9
4♠	All Pass			◊ K 9 6 2
^ Limit raise				♣ Q 9 3
Opening Lead: ♣ A				

East
♠ 9 7 3
♡ K 10 7 5 2
◊ J 8 4
♣ 10 4

West leads the ♣AK, then the ♣7.

South follows with the ♣5 and 6. East ruffs the third club as declarer follows with the 8.

What should East return at Trick 4? Does the ♣7 carry any suit preference? The ♣J2 are still out. Did you select the ♡5 or the ◊4?

Or other? Is it time to be busy or quiet?

If you returned any red card, declarer made the contract. Only a passive trump return defeats four spades.

West ♠ 8
♡ J 8 6 3
◊ Q 7 3
♣ A K J 7 2

South
♠ A K J 5 4
♡ Q 4
◊ A 10 5
♣ 8 6 5

A heart return away from the king is into the A9 opposite Q4. A diamond return allows declarer to play the diamond suit for four tricks, discarding his heart loser.

A passive trump return means declarer left on his own has to lose at least one more trick.

Deal 104. Getting a Step Ahead

West	North	East	South
1♡	P	2♡	3♠^
All Pass			

^ Intermediate

Opening Lead: ♡ 10

♠ 9 6 4
♡ Q 6 2
◊ K 10 3
♣ 10 4 3 2

East
♠ J 8 7
♡ A J 7
◊ J 9 7
♣ 8 7 6 5

The ♡10 won Trick 1. West continued the ♡4 to East's ♡J. How should East continue the defense?

East continued a passive defense with the ♡A, ruffed by declarer. After drawing trumps declarer led the ♣J from his hand losing to West's ♣Q. West played the ◊2. Declarer won in hand with the ◊A and led the ♣K from hand.

West won the ♣A and played another low diamond. Declarer won in dummy with the ◊K and discarded his diamond loser on the ♣10. Making three spades, losing two hearts and two clubs.

How would you asses the blame?

What's often the best defense against a second suit? Entry removal. East knows the third heart is going to be ruffed. After winning the second heart, East must shift to a diamond, attacking dummy's entry.

The timing now is in favor of the defenders. Declarer does not have time to set up the clubs.

West
♠ 2
♡ K 10 9 8 4
◊ Q 6 5 2
♣ A Q 9

South
♠ A K Q 10 5 3
♡ 5 3
◊ A 8 4
♣ K J

Deal 105. Right Idea, Wrong Suit

South	West	North	East
3♡	P	4♡	All Pass

♠ 8 5 2
♡ K 9 5
◊ K 8
♣ A J 8 5 2

Opening Lead: ◊ 5

East
♠ Q 10 3
♡ 7 4
◊ A Q 6 2
♣ K Q 10 6

East won the first two diamond tricks.
How should East continue at Trick 3?

East shifted to the ♠3, an aggressive play, assuming he had dummy's club suit under control. Declarer won the ♠A and led a club to dummy's ♣A. He ruffed a club high, played a middle trump to dummy's ♡9 and ruffed another club high.

A middle trump to the ♡K and another club ruff followed. The last club was good and having preserved a low heart in hand, the ♡5 was the entry.
Making four hearts.

So much for having the club suit under control. What could East have done?

Timing. Return a trump at Trick 3. The defense would then be a step ahead in the timing. Declarer lacks the entries to ruff three clubs and return to dummy.
Down one.

West ♠ K J 7 6
♡ 8
◊ 10 9 7 5 3
♣ 7 4 3

South
♠ A 9 4
♡ A Q J 10 6 3 2
◊ J 4
♣ 9

Yes, it's often correct to try to set up your trick(s) in the side suit, but entry problems take priority.

131

Deal 106. Better Hurry Up

	North	East	South	West
♠ A Q	1 NT	P	2♡^	P
♡ J 9 6 4	2♠	P	3♡	P
◊ K 7 4 3	4♡		All Pass	
♣ A J 3				

^ A Jacoby transfer to spades

Opening Lead: ◊ Queen

West
♠ 6 5
♡ K Q 2
◊ Q J 10 8
♣ K 10 7 6

The ◊Q wins Trick 1 and declarer ruffs the diamond continuation. Declarer plays the ♠7 to the ace and finesses the ♡J to West's ♡Q. Now what?

How should West continue?

West played another diamond. Declarer ruffed and played the ♡A. He continued playing spades. West could ruff in, but declarer was in control.

After cashing the ♣A, he discarded two clubs from dummy on his spades and ruffed the last club from his hand in dummy.

How could West have played differently?

At Trick 2, West needed to get active with a club switch, hoping to set up a trick if partner had the ♣Q. Otherwise, as happened, declarer had time to draw trumps and discard dummy's clubs on his spades.

East
♠ 8 4 3 2
♡ 5
◊ A 6 5 2
♣ Q 9 8 4

South
♠ K J 10 9 7
♡ A 10 8 7 3
◊ 9
♣ 5 2

132

Deal 107. A Worthwhile Trade

North	East	South	West
3◊	P	3NT	All Pass

Opening Lead: ♡ J

♠ A 5
♡ 7 5
◊ K J 10 9 8 7 3
♣ 9 2

♠ K 10 4 3 2
♡ 9 6 4 3
◊ A Q
♣ Q 7

Declarer won Trick 1 with the ♡K and led a diamond to the jack. After winning the ◊Q, how should East continue the defense?

East returned a passive heart. Declarer won and led his last diamond. East won, but declarer had at least nine tricks.

At the other table in a team game, her counterpart had gone down. How?

Play started the same, but after East won the first diamond, she returned the spade king. Declarer had no winning options. If he won, he had no entry to the diamonds. If he ducked, East would just play another spade.

Declarer took no diamond tricks and had to play clubs out of his hand.

No 3NT for this declarer.

West
♠ 9 8 6
♡ J 10 8 2
◊ 5 2
♣ A 10 8 4

South
♠ Q J 7
♡ A K Q
◊ 6 4
♣ K J 6 5 3

"Good trade, partner," said West. "Giving them three spades, but no diamonds."

Deal 108. Can You Stop Him?

South	West	North	East
1♡	P	1♠	P
1NT	P	3NT	All Pass

♠ K Q J 8 6
♡ 8 4
◊ 6 5 2
♣ K Q 7

Opening Lead: ◊ 9

East
♠ A 9 3
♡ 5 3
◊ A 10 4 3
♣ A J 8 3

East won the opening lead with the ◊A and returned a passive diamond three. Do you agree?

How would you have continued the defense?

East will get back in with one of his aces to play another diamond and establish his long diamond. East takes two diamonds, one club, and one spade holding declarer to nine tricks.

Was there a better defense to defeat 3NT?

East could keep declarer from the spades by holding up once, but the clubs were the problem. East needed to try to remove the club entries. At Trick 2, a low club would not suffice as West may not have the ♣10. In that case, declarer would win the ♣10 in hand.

At Trick 2, East must shift to the ♣J. Declarer will have no winning options and will only take one spade trick. Nine tricks are not possible after that defense.

West
♠ 7 5 2
♡ Q 10 7 6
◊ 9 8 7
♣ 6 5 2

South
♠ 10 4
♡ A K J 9 2
◊ K Q J
♣ 10 9 4

Deal 109. Another Wooden Soldier

East	South	West	North	♠ A Q 10 7 5
P	1◊	1♡	1♠	♡ A 7
P	2◊	P	3♣	◊ Q 8
P	3NT	All Pass		♣ 10 8 3 2

East
♠ 8 3
♡ J 8 3
◊ A 7 5 3
♣ K J 9 6

Opening Lead: ♡ 4

Declarer won the opening lead in dummy with the ♡A and led the ◊Q. East jumped up with the ◊A (a good play).

How should the defense continue?

East returned the ♡J, (not such a good play). Declarer claimed twelve tricks!

East tried to grab West's hand. "What did you have for your bid?" he asked.

"It doesn't matter," replied West. "You had them beat if you didn't woodenly return my suit."

South is surely marked with the ♡K. If he had the ♡Q, he likely would have ducked the opening lead to insure two heart tricks.

East must switch to a club, the ♣K then the ♣6, thus created a surrounding play, the ♣J9 over the ♣108. The defense takes four club tricks. Down one.

West
♠ 9 6 4 2
♡ Q 10 5 4 2
◊ 6
♣ A 5 4

South
♠ K J
♡ K 9 6
◊ K J 10 9 4 2
♣ Q 7

Deal 110. The Race is On

South	West	North	East	♠ 9 8 7	
1♡	P	2♡	4◊	♡ 6 4 3	
4♡	Dbl	All Pass		◊ J 5	East
				♣ A Q 10 7 2	♠ Q 5

Opening Lead: ◊ 3   ♡ 8

East won Trick 1 as declarer followed   ◊ A K 10 9 7 6 4

with the ◊2. How should East continue?   ♣ J 8 5

East continued another high diamond. Declarer ruffed and warned of a probable 4-1 trump split led the ♡2. West won the ♡9 and seeing no future in diamonds since declarer could now ruff in dummy, switched to a low spade.

The race was on. Declarer won East's ♠Q with the ace and led the ♡5. West won the ♡10 and continued spades. But declarer was in control.

He won the ♠K, drew trumps, and ran the clubs to discard his low spades. The yelling started. "Why did you double?" screamed East. "My bid didn't promise any defense." "Down one," said West, "If you knew how to defend."

Who was to blame? How would you have defended?

A passive forcing defense shortening declarer's trumps wasn't going to be effective since declarer could ruff diamonds in dummy. This was a race against a second suit; set up a spade trick for the defense before declarer set up clubs.

If East shifts to a spade at Trick 2, the defense is a step ahead and wins the race.

I'd blame West for doubling. That made it too difficult for East to find a spade switch, being worried West's lead was a singleton, easier without the double.

West	♠ J 10 6 2	
	♡ Q J 10 9	
	◊ Q 8 3	
	♣ 9 6	South
		♠ A K 4 3
		♡ A K 7 5 2
		◊ 2
		♣ K 4 3

Deal 111. Nothing to Lose

	♠ A 6	South	West	North	East
	♡ J 10 3	1♡	P	2◊	P
	◊ K Q J 10 7	2♡	P	3♡	P
West	♣ J 10 3	4♡	All Pass		
♠ K 5 3					
♡ 8 5 2			Opening Lead: ♣ A		
◊ A 8 3					
♣ A K 7 2					

West led the ♣A and East played a discouraging ♣4.

How should West continue the defense?

West knew by counting the HCP that East was broke. Maybe he could give East a diamond ruff? He cashed the ◊A and played a second diamond.

Declarer scored six heart tricks, four diamond tricks, and one spade.
Eleven tricks.

Any better ideas? That defense wasn't very effective.

Yes, partner is broke. But there is room in his hand for a queen. That's a better option than a singleton. How about switching to a spade? Is that dangerous?

No, once West takes his diamond ace, declarer is discarding everything anyhow.
It's now or never; an active spade switch before giving up the diamond ace. East does have the spade queen. When West wins the diamond ace, the defense has four tricks. If not, West probably wasn't going to score his ♠K anyway.
Down one.

	East
	♠ Q 10 9 7 4 2
South	♡ 6
♠ J 8	◊ 9 4
♡ A K Q 9 7 4	♣ 9 8 6 4
◊ 6 5 2	
♣ Q 5	

Looking at all those winners in dummy, it can't hurt to try something.

Deal 112. Me Too, Nothing to Lose

South	West	North	East	♠ J 7 5
1◊	P	3◊^	P	♡ Q
3♠	P	5◊	All Pass	◊ K 8 6 4
^ Invitational				♣ K J 10 9 7 East
Opening Lead: ♡ J				♠ K 2
				♡ A K 8 4 2
				◊ 10 3
				♣ A Q 5 4

East won Trick 1 with the ♡K. Knowing partner was broke, he chose a passive defense. If declarer had two clubs, the contract was going down.

How would you defend as East?

East returned the ♡A at Trick 2. Declarer ruffed and led the ♣8. East won and was finished. After drawing trumps, declarer set up the club suit with a ruffing finesse and discarded his spades.

Was there a successful defense?

East needed West to hold the ♠Q. If declarer had ♠AQ, his king was not taking a trick anyhow. Lead the ♠2, not the ♠K, as declarer, fearing a singleton, may panic and rise with the ♠A at Trick 2. This has everything to gain and nothing to lose.

Home run! Down one.

West
♠ Q 6 4 3
♡ J 10 6 3
◊ 9 7
♣ 6 3 2

           South
           ♠ A 10 9 8
           ♡ 9 7 5
           ◊ A Q J 5 2
           ♣ 8

Deal 113. Not So Safe

An interesting deal from the 1972 Bridge World reprinted in 2022.
Presented by long-time Swiss star Jean Besse.

		South	West	North	East
♠ 8 4 2		South	West	North	East
♡ A K 5		1♡	Dbl	Redbl	P
◊ A J 3		P	1♠	P	P
♣ 8 7 4 2		2◊	P	4♡	All Pass

West
♠ A Q 10 3
♡ 8 7
◊ 9 4 2
♣ A K 5 3

(as bid in pre-1972)
Opening Lead: ♣ A

Trick 1 went ♣A; deuce, queen, six. How should West continue?

West continued with a safe-looking ♣K. Declarer ruffed, played a low diamond to dummy and ruffed another club. Then another low diamond to dummy followed by ruffing the last club.

Declarer drew trumps and cashed two more diamonds for ten tricks; a very nice dummy reversal.

Could this have been prevented?

West can infer East does not have four spades or he certainly would have bid them over the redouble. Declarer, with at least three spades must be 3=5=4=1.

With no high club, declarer must have ♠K, ♡QJ, ◊KQ for his opening one-bid.

With a trump return at Trick 2, declarer will be short one dummy entry to execute his plan.

East
♠ J 7 5
♡ 6 4 2
◊ 10 8 5
♣ Q J 10 9

South
♠ K 9 6
♡ Q J 10 9 3
◊ K Q 7 6
♣ 6

Deal 114. Careful

East	South	West	North	♠ A J	
1♣	P	1♠	Dbl	♡ A Q J 3	
Redbl^	P	P	2◊	◊ K Q J 10 4	
P	2♡	P	4♡	♣ K 5	East
All Pass					♠ K 9 5
^ Three spades					♡ 8 4 2
Opening Lead: ♣ 10					◊ A 3
					♣ A Q 9 4 3

East won the opening lead with the ♣Q. How should the defense proceed?

East saw three defensive tricks, maybe fewer once declarer sets up the diamonds. He cashed the ♣A, everyone followed. The only hope seemed to be a spade trick. He switched to the ♠5.

Was this the right defense? Why?

Yes, that second suit is coming home, and the defenders need a spade trick. If declarer has the ♠Q, declarer is going to knock out East's ◊A and discard his spade losers. But East's active switch is one trick too late? Why?

What card is declarer known to have for sure? Yes, the ♣J. By cashing the second club, what has East done? East has set up the ♣J for declarer to pitch dummy's ♠J. By Yogi's calculations, the probability that South had the ♣J was 140%. East had to NOT cash the second club, but switch to a spade at Trick 2.

```
West    ♠ Q 10 7 3 2
        ♡ 9
        ◊ 8 7 6 5 2
        ♣ 10 7        South
                      ♠ 8 6 4
                      ♡ K 10 7 6 5
                      ◊ 9
                      ♣ J 8 6 2
```

Deal 115. The Opening Lead

East	South	West	North	♠ Q J 9
1♣	1♠	P	2♣	♡ A Q J 6 3
P	2♠	P	4♠	◊ 8 6
	All Pass			♣ A Q 10

East
♠ A 6
♡ K 10
◊ Q J 10 2
♣ K J 8 5 4

Opening Lead: ♣ 7

At Trick 1, declarer played low, East won the jack as South followed with the ♣6. How should East continue the defense?

East continued with a passive ◊Q. Declarer won the ◊A and drew trumps, knocking out the ♠A. East continued with the ◊J. South won the ◊K and took a losing heart finesse. He discarded his remaining losers on dummy's hearts.

He lost one spade, one heart, and one club. Making four hearts.

Where did East think a fourth trick was coming from?

Declarer must have the ◊AK for his overcall along with the ♠K. Think back to the opening lead, the ♣7. From what? The 9, 3, and 2 are missing. Can West have three? No, not 973 or 972 or 97 or 732. He must have started with 7 or 7x.

At Trick 2, instead of a passive ◊Q, throw the ♣K (suit preference for hearts) into the teeth of dummy's ♣AQ. Win the first trump and give partner a club ruff. Down one.

West
♠ 5 3 2
♡ 8 7 4 2
◊ 9 5 4 3
♣ 7 3

South
♠ K 10 8 7 4
♡ 9 5
◊ A K 7
♣ 9 6 2

141

Deal 116. Four Kings

North	East	South	West	♠ A J 4	
1♣	P	1♠	P	♡ 7 5 3	
1NT	P	2◊^	P	◊ A 6 3	
3♠#	P	4♠	All Pass	♣ A J 10 9	East

^ Artificial and forcing

\# Maximum with three spades

Opening Lead: ♡ 2

East
♠ K 8
♡ K J 4
◊ K 10 9 2
♣ K 6 4 2

How should East defend?

East played the ♡K at Trick 1 losing to the ace. Declarer next let the ♠10 ride losing to East's ♠K. East returned the ♡J, losing to declarer's ♡Q.

Declarer finished the trumps and lost a club finesse. The defense cashed a heart, but declarer's diamond losers went on dummy's good clubs.

How could East have known continuing a passive heart defense was hopeless?

At Trick 1, East should make a discovery play by putting up the ♡J, not the ♡K. When declarer wins the ♡Q, East will know he needs at least one diamond trick.

After winning the ♠K, a shift to the ◊10 defeats the contract.

West
♠ 7 6 2
♡ 10 9 6 2
◊ Q 8 5
♣ 7 5 3

South
♠ Q 10 9 5 3
♡ A Q 8
◊ J 7 4
♣ Q 8

Printed in the United States
by Baker & Taylor Publisher Services